Walks in Yorkshire: The North East, Comprising Redcar, Saltburn, Whitby, Etc., and the Moors and Dales Between the Tees, the Derwent, the Vale of York and the Sea

William Stott Banks

WALKS IN YORKSHIRE:

N. E.

WAKEFIELD:

PRINTED BY W. R. HALL, KIRKGATE.

O

WALKS IN YORKSHIRE;

THE NORTH EAST,

COMPRISING

REDCAR, SALTBURN,

WHITBY, SCARBOROUGH AND FILEY,

WITH INTERVENING PLACES; AND

THE MOORS AND DALES

BETWEEN

THE TEES, THE DERWENT, THE VALE OF YORK

AND THE SEA,

BY

W. S. BANKS.

LONDON : J. RUSSELL SMITH, SOHO SQUARE.

WAKEFIELD : W. R. HALL, KIRKGATE.

—

1866.

Kyng Davyd hee stode on the rising hille,
  And the verdante prospecte view'd;
And he sawe that sweete river that o'er the moore
  Roll'd on her sylver floode.

BATTLE OF CUTON MOORE.

These cliffs, that never seem to move,
  Are worn through base and brow;
The rains distress them from above,
  The ocean from below.

A Talk on Filey Brig.—ARTHUR MUNBY.

CONTENTS.

4.

5.

6.

7.

8.

FILEY TO HACKNESS AND CROSS CLIFF; SALTERSGATE
TO LILHOE CROSS AND SLEIGHTS; CAWTHORN
CAMPS, PICKERING.

9.

THE HOWARDIAN HILLS FROM CASTLE HOWARD TO
CRAYKE.

CORRECTIONS.

Page 59, line 29, for *Mr.* read *Dr.*

„ 92, „ 22, for *Flying* read **Fyling**.

INTRODUCTION.

OUR great county of York, which covers nearly 6000 square miles of land and has at least two millions of inhabitants, is not only divided arbitrarily for political, judicial and other like purposes, but has natural divisions of a distinct and remarkable kind. The land is mountainous in part, hilly in other parts, and elsewhere is spread out in great plains. It exhibits, moreover, much variety in the character and conditions of its people, who speak many dialects and employ themselves in many different ways. They are (stating the matter broadly) agriculturists, manufacturers, miners, fishermen, commercial and seafaring folk.

From the river Tees, southward throughout the county, extends the great Vale of York, sixty miles long and from twelve to twenty six broad, down which the chief part of the drainage flows,

B 2

nearly all our principal rivers pouring their streams into it.

West of the great vale lie the huge fells that fill the space between the Upper Tees, the boundaries of Westmorland and North Lancashire, and the Ribble, the Aire and the Wharfe, comprising our greatest mountains, the highest of which (Mickle fell) is 2596 feet o.s. above the sea; and, south of these, the hills between the Wharfe and the borders of Cheshire and Derbyshire.

On the eastern side are, first, the Vale of Cleveland, and the north-eastern moors, ranging in height from nearly 1500 down to 300 or 200 feet, their chief stream, the Esk, flowing east to the sea. Next is the Vale of Pickering which stretches from the foot of the Hambletons near Coxwold to the coast at Filey, and has at its widest part a breadth of eight miles. This vale has it own river system, consisting of becks that drain the moors and then become affluents of the Derwent. South of this are the Wolds, the highest point whereof (808 feet o.s.) is about seven miles east of the Derwent at Stamford bridge; and last comes the district of Holderness the several parts of which lie at slight elevations above the encroaching sea, the figures on the maps ranging generally from about eighty feet down to ten and less, and the greatest height being given as 159 feet.

The following is Professor Phillips's table of

the several districts above described, given in
his *Rivers Mountains and Sea Coast of Yorkshire*
published in 1855 :—

Cleveland [vale]

NORTH WESTERN		NORTH EASTERN
HILLS.		HILLS.
Ribblesdale.	Vale of York.	Vale of Pickering.
SOUTH WESTERN		SOUTH EASTERN
HILLS.		HILLS.

Holderness.

The present series of walks relates to the Vale
of Cleveland and the North-eastern moors and
Sea coast. In Baines's *Flora of Yorkshire, page
xii.*, the edge of the moors is described as
looking with greater boldness over the Vale of
York, from the abrupt heights of Hambleton,
than any one, acquainted only with the southern
oolites, could imagine. "The highest point of
the district is at Burton Head [six miles south-
east of Stokesley], and the general slope is to the
south-east. In this direction as well as toward
the north it reaches the sea and thus on three
sides its boundary is a cliff, while on the south
side it declines gently into the Vale of Pickering.
The waters run for the most part to the south
through various dales and collect in the river

Derwent; but one considerable stream, the Esk, runs eastward to Whitby. The hills derive importance from their abruptness and the valleys are interesting from the narrow woody and secluded character of their lower parts. The strata comprise the Lias clays and interposed calcareous and arenaceous beds, the oolitic limestones, and about 700 feet of sandstones shales and thin bad coal. One great basaltic dyke crosses the district from the Tees to near Robin Hood's bay. The greater portion of the higher ground is covered by heath and peat. The interior valleys become woody in their lower parts, but the sea air checks the growth of trees on the coast, in all but well-defended spots like the sheltered banks of the Esk. An aspect of peculiar desolation belongs to the dark and wearisome moorlands which fill the immense area between Scarborough, Whitby, Stokesley and Helmsley."

Notwithstanding the elevated and bold character of the moors in this district we find no such huge, steep, rugged, and distinctly separated fells, rising more than 2000 feet above the sea, as constitute the high ground of north-western Yorkshire. The moors, as may be gathered from the above extract, are wide spaces, and the valleys are, comparatively, few and narrow.

The following tables of some characteristics of those parts of the north-east into which the present walks extend are Professor Phillips's, the words in brackets being added by me.

[The Vale of] Cleveland.

1. Greatest Elevation—generally below 300 feet. Rosebury Topping, a detached hill of the north-eastern district is [1057 feet O.S.]
2. The Principal Streams are branches of the Leven.
3. Average Depth of Rain in a year at Upleatham, 22 inches, [at Redcar, 1862-4, nearly 20 inches.]
4. Geological Constitution—lias and new red formations much overspread by "northern drift."
5. Valuable Minerals, &c.,—alum shale, ironstone, whinstone, gravel.

North Eastern [Moorlands.]

1. Greatest Elevation—[1489 feet O.S.] in Burton Head.
2. Principal Rivers which rise in the district—Esk, Wisk, Derwent.
3. Average Depth of Rain in a year at Brandsby, 28½ inches.
4. Geological Constitution—Oolitic and lias formations.
5. Valuable Minerals, &c.,—coal, ironstone, alum shale, jet, building stone, cement stone, whinstone, peat.
6. Dialect—The high grounds [are] called ["Moors;"] the valleys receive the names of "Dales" and "Gills;" the rivulets are called "Becks;" the waterfalls ["Fosses;"] Tumuli [and mound-like elevations] "Howes;" a stone or heap of stones is sometimes called "Man," [also "Rook;"] abrupt hill-edges are "Nabs [and "Banks;" projecting sea cliffs, "Nabs" and "Nesses;" inlets of the sea are called "Wykes."]

The Vale of Pickering, though perhaps it ought, strictly speaking, to be considered as out of the north-eastern district, may also be here included, thus—

VALE OF PICKERING.

1. GREATEST ELEVATION generally below 100 feet.
2. THE DERWENT is the great drain of the vale.
3. AVERAGE DEPTH OF RAIN in a year at Scarborough, 23 inches; [in 1862-4, 19·22 inches; at Malton 1862-4, 25·66 inches.]
4. GEOLOGICAL CONSTITUTION — Kimmeridge clay, covered by lacustrine and river sediments.
5. DIALECT—The low grounds are called "Marshes," or "Marishes."

For a fuller account of the several matters contained in this introduction, the reader may profitably refer to Professor Phillips's *Rivers, Mountains and Sea Coast of Yorkshire*, above mentioned.

In the following pages "I," of course, means the writer only; "we" refers to the writer and another or others.

I.

CLEVELAND; UPPER ESKDALE; OVER MOORS TO LEVISHAM STATION.

Margery Moorpoot—Canny Yatton—Changes in speech —Cleveland; boundaries, productions, history, Captain Cook, the vale—Stokesley—Rosebury—Homes and graves of Brigantes—Easby moor Obelisk—Kildale —Westerdale—Castleton—Danby dale end—Lealholm bridge—Glaisdale end—Beggar's bridge—Egton bridge and country round—British village—Vale of Murk Esk—Julian park—Roman way—Cinder hill—Mauley cross—Levisham station—Pickering beck.

HAVING taken up the maps of North Eastern Yorkshire, after spending a considerable time among the fells and dales of the North West, we felt a little uncertainty about the best plan for our walks in this district. A first journey is always open to doubt; but, if we go at all, it is necessary to begin somewhere, and so we decide upon starting off with Rosebury Topping in Cleveland, that sweet green cone, in childhood associated with Margery Moorpoot and a broad north-Yorkshire dialect, supposed to be spoken by men and women with laughing mouths opening from ear to ear across great red cheeks; but, sad to say, our little-boy's dream will not come true; nobody will, as a matter of course, call Ayton "Canny Yatton," though many still think Rosebury "t'biggest hill i' all Yorkshur, aboon a mahle an a hawf heegh an as cawd as ice at t' top on't i' t'yattest day i' summer," which it is not; nor will any peculiarity of face be seen, nor the farmers be found, in any sense, "bumpkins," but shrewd men. And, if they be somewhat noisy in their mirth, as healthy, hearty Yorkshiremen have a prescriptive right to be, they can, as I gratefully remember, be considerate of other people's comfort in their jollity. Supposing the personages of the North Yorkshire tales ever were representative, as one hopes they were in some respects, they have, in regard to gross oddities at least, ceased to be so; and the persons we meet at inns and in cottages and on the roads in the Vale of Cleveland, speak a plain Yorkshire speech, which has its pecularity, but which does not seem absurd to a West Yorkshire-man. Schooling, quick travelling, and more frequent intercourse with other places and people are bringing about changes all over the county. Few persons in my town, for example, now talk their mother tongue with that propriety which would have been expected of a native thirty years ago; and even suburban places, which in the last generation were noteworthy for the strength of their dialect, are clipping off the sharp points that made what they said so forcible, and rounding their speech into national English. In the least accessible places of the north-east, like Runswick and Staithes and remote villages in the dales, however, many characteristics, both of speech and manners, exist now, which probably existed fifty years ago.

Cleveland, which consists of both hills and plain, though popularly believed to have low lands only, is bounded by the Tees and sea coast from near Newstead hall, two and a half miles above Yarm, to East Row beck the same distance north-west of Whitby; then by this beck for a mile inland, whence the boundary, turning south, crosses Swarth howe to the Esk opposite Sleights; follows the Esk and the Murk Esk and the beck below Hazle head to Wheeldale howe; runs westward along the high tops of the moors, Shunner howe, Loose howe, White cross, Ralph cross and Flat howe, and by Stoney ridge over Burton head; continues by Hasty bank, Cold-moor end and Cringley moor; bends south at Carlton bank for above two miles; again goes west over Arncliffe, north of Mount Grace, and down the Wisk, and then turns round Appleton up to the Tees again—thus taking in a good deal of moor land and sea coast, beside the broad level of the Cleveland vale. The Tees limit is perhaps eighteen miles long; the coast line about twenty; and the rest, forming an irregular

curve, not less than forty-five.   The breadth is
generally about twelve miles.   This is a picturesque and valuable tract of country ; has lands
good for farming ; fine woods ; much ironstone
and alum shale — the former fast altering the
aspect of many parts — numerous country
mansions, villages and towns ; an enterprising
fishing population ; places for sea side visitors ;
at least one very large centre of iron smelting—
Middlesbrough — two or three alum works ;
passenger and mineral railways completed and
in progress.   It is now more interesting to
holiday tourists than it probably will be after
further development of its mineral wealth, when
others of the hitherto quiet dales shall be busy
with iron furnaces and black with their smoke.

Cleveland has, of course, histories of old times
and people ; records of successive possessors of
the soil, Britons, Romans, Saxons and Danes,
and of remarkable places and personages in later
days.   Its priories or abbeys were Guisbrough,
Grosmont, Bazedale ; castles, Mulgrave, Danby,
Skelton, Kilton and others.   In the times of the
Norman kings the family whose name is now
spelt Bruce, which has been spelt thirty different
ways, owned Skelton, founded Guisbrough priory,
and are said to have tried the compatibility of
religious exercises with business by holding their
weekly markets after morning service on
Sundays.   Among the worthiest men of old
times Mr. Tweddell, in his *Bards and Authors*

of Cleveland, South Durham and the Vicinage,
claims to place Cedmon,

> "........ the humble herdsman of the swine
> That fed on mast of Cleveland's oaks and beeches,"

afterward Cedmon the monk of Streoneshalh,
who sang "the origin of things;" Gower the
friend of Chaucer, though he was but born in the
"Archdeaconry;" and Roger Ascham, Queen
Elizabeth's tutor, who was almost a Cleveland
man, being born at Kirkby Wisk in 1515. The
most notable Cleveland worthy of late years was
Captain James Cook the circumnavigator, born
at Marton, of whose father, a venerable man
living at Redcar, Mr. Tweddell, in the Redcar
Handbook, repeats the story from Colman,
mentioned by Mr. Ord (p. 384) that, two or
three years before the old man's eightieth
summer, he learned to read, that he might
peruse his son's first voyage round the world,
which statement is, however, scarcely consistent
with what Mr. Ord (p. 413) says of the same
man's composing a long inscription for his family
tombstone in Ayton (?) church yard, and probably
cutting the letters with his own hand.

The Vale of Cleveland, a branch of the great
Vale of York, is a plain of fertile arable and
meadow lands, tilled by good farmers, and is
bounded on the north-west and north-east by the
Tees and the sea, and on the south-east by the
hills, the slopes of which make an inward sweep
from Arncliffe round by Carlton, Busby, Kirkby

and Burton banks, Ingleby-Greenhow, Easby moor, Rosebury, and the spur over Pinchin-thorp, to within a mile and a half of Guisbrough town. Stokesley and Ayton lie in this curve, the former four to six miles from the bases of the hills. The bordering moorlands, varying in height from 600 or 700 to over 1400 feet, are intersected by narrow dales carrying little streams to the river Leven—pronounced *leev'n*, probably the Celtic word *llevn*, smooth. This is a small stream, flowing west out of Kildale by Ayton and Stokesley to the Tees near Yarm. Going up the great vale by Thirsk and Northallerton to Picton, we pass at three or four miles distance, first the Hambletons and then the Cleveland hills, and the north-western faces of the latter are nearer still after turning eastward at Picton.

We went to Stokesley expecting to be in the midst of ironworkings and smoke, but found neither. The people live by farming and are as quiet as in Hutton's days, 1808, having time now as then to lean, as he said, against walls and settle the affairs of the nation. Stokesley is a pleasant town of one long, wide, street with open spaces; not regular, but with buildings on the whole good, chiefly brick. Among its worthy things is the Preston school, endowed by a local solicitor, wherein about thirty boys of all sects are taught for a nominal charge. Near Stokesley is Busby hall, about which Hutton, in his trip to Coatham, tells the story, alluded to by Sisson in his historic

sketch of Wakefield church, of the grandmother
of Mr. Strawbenzie, keeper to 1816 of the West
Riding House of Correction, who passed by her
daughter and left her property to a distant
relative. At the foot of Rosebury, which is four
miles from Stokesley, we cross the basaltic dyke,
locally *flint*, which is here, as all along when
accessible, as at Castleton, Egton bridge and
elsewhere, worked for road making.

The ascent of Rosebury—by Camden called
Ounsbery, *Odin's*bery (?)—is easy. The top is
only about 670 feet above the village of Newton
at its base, or 1057 above the sea. Short grass.
grows almost to the top, but the summit is a cap-
of soft freestone. It is singularly pointed as seen
from all sides but the south-east, for in the slack.
of Ayton moor, above Lonsdale, its conical form
is not so apparent because of our looking to the.
slope that joins it to Easby moor. From the
top we view the large plains in Yorkshire and
Durham, drained by the Swale and the Tees,
from the north-western hills to the Tees mouth,
Guisbrough and Arncliffe, dotted with villages.
and farms, alternately meadow and arable, and
on which also lie the large and smoky towns of
Darlington, Stockton and Middlesbrough. The
smaller moors of Barnaby (Eston nab) Wilton
and Thornton lie half way between us and the
lower Tees. Eastward, beyond Coatham and
Redcar, is the sea and, over Guisbrough, the
comparatively high cliffs about Saltburn ; whilst

southward lie the moors, some of the spurs of which, named above, project into the Vale of Cleveland. Twenty or thirty yards from the top of Rosebury, on the northern face, is the site of an oft-mentioned British village, the tenants whereof doubtless drank at the spring coming from the summit and buried their worthiest dead under the tumuli upon the adjoining moors. Passing from Rosebury along the Hutton, Great Ayton, Easby and Coates moors to Kildale village we met with many of these tumuli mostly opened and left open. We put the question to ourselves whether it was right to turn out these last resting places of the old people and leave them exposed? And, even after reading the chapter on Tumuli in Mr. Lubbock's "Pre-Historic Times," I think the mounds ought always to be re-heaped, the fact of their examination being indicated by some mark. The north-eastern moors were the homes of great numbers of the Brigantes, for almost everywhere on the heights are found the sites of their dwellings, and their burial places.

Upon Easby moor stands a hollow obelisk, erected in memory of Captain Cook, by the late Mr. Campion of Whitby, who tells the captain's virtues and the times and places of his birth and death on three iron plates, at a length wearisome to read when the cold winds are sweeping over the moor. Desisting when half through the inscription we turned to look toward Ayton, where Cook first went to school, and Marton his birthplace, which lies six miles off in the direction of Middlesbrough—the little thatched house he was born in was (they say) pulled down years ago. The views from Easby moor, as from Rosebury, are fine, and particularly so down the wooded banks of Coates moor into Kildale and along the Cleveland railway by Sleddale beck toward the dale of the river Esk. The latter beck, which rises near Rosebury, and the streams out of Bazedale and Westerdale unite near Castleton and thenceforward take the one name Esk.

Our course from Kildale lay over the moors by Westwood into a wild and deep part of Bazedale, where the beck is fringed with straggling patches of trees, past Slaethorn park —Sloethorn, sounded *Slaytron*—into Westerdale, which has plenty of trees and two becks, one carrying with it the name " Esk." The chapel and Mr. Duncombe's shooting house that looks like a castle, are striking objects as we approach the place. Near the church are the remains of a British village, but many of the once numerous pits have been ploughed up. The fanciful, retired-Sailor's pillar (Thomas Bulmer's) put up in 1727, with its inscribed words and carved ships' hulls, stands in a yard opposite the pits. The land in this and the other dales of the Esk grows good corn and grass, and feeds horned cattle and sheep well. We only saw Danby dale from High Castleton. On the opposite moors between Danby beacon and Wapley are the remains of British dwellings mentioned in a subsequent walk. About a mile north of Danby dale end poor coal is got and "white flints." At Pepper bridge in Castleton is a bank of old slag from ironworks, one of several believed to have been left there by the Romans. The farmers occupy from thirty to a hundred acres, averaging seventy or eighty, only odd ones reaching 200. Castleton—so named from the castle which stood on the mound over the river — is a little town about twelve miles from Stokesley by the usual road, but more the way we went.

The road down the dale, taking the south side, winds about with the Esk, and rises and falls continually. At Dale end the scenery is striking, several moors appearing to break off there ; and in other places we see the same, especially at Glaisdale end where the moor ends come crowding down, as it were, to the river, the steep banks clothed with trees or pushing bold heads above them, and the deep, narrow, dales filled with foliage. Little and Great Fryopdales, rounded hollows having more or less wood, lie between Danby dale end and Glaisdale. At Lealholm bridge the banks of the stream are splendidly wooded, Crunkley gill being a "singularly abrupt and wooded chasm of about a mile in length through which the river Esk forces its impetuous course." From Glaisdale

end to the level of the river at Beggar's bridge
the road passes along the steep banks, and at
each turn changes to a view more bold or
beautiful, as we think, than that which preceded
it.   The foot bridge over the Esk, called the
Beggar's bridge, is well known to Whitby visitors
who go there along the stream from Egton
bridge.   Mrs. George Dawson has written some
nice verses on it, which we were glad to read
again in the locality.   In due course we arrived
at the Horse Shoe at Egton bridge.   Underwood,
the keeper of the inn, was born at this house,
and so were his father and grandfather.   They
have been here, Under-*arncliffe*-woods, for, they
say, 200 years.

The country all around Egton bridge is
especially fine.   The Arncliffe woods and Limber
hill, Egton town hill, and the uneven grounds
down to Grosmont, with Goadland dale to Beck
hole, Goadland moors, and the banks that lie
between Egton bridge and the Delves and
Swinstey on the road to Pickering, are a puzzle
which require plenty of time to trace out.   From
Arncliffe wood top are excellent views, and so
there are going up to and at Egton grange.   All
the banks overlooking the lower part of Esk
valley, with the contiguous moors forward to the
sea cliffs at Whitby Laiths and the sea beyond,
lie open to view from these places.   The British
village at the grange, lying in a corner on the
moor top, above the village of Delves, and

C 2

between east and west Arncliffe wood, has a like extensive prospect. The site of this, marked "pits" on the Ordnance map, and the road to it are fenced from the surrounding land. The inclosure may be said to represent, roughly, a figure 8 with the centre line removed and two slits in the ends for the road in and out. It is now perhaps 500 feet long and nearly as wide, but part was taken into an adjoining field some years ago. There are many scores of pits more or less accurately rounded, varying from eight or nine to eighteen or twenty feet in diameter, and from three to six feet deep, having a space through the midst for the road. The village stands above the ground on all sides so that no water could drain in, and on the south-west boundary and, along part of the north-eastern face, run banks, apparently in part artificial, and, outside the first, a broad level as if made for a road or other purpose. The pits are not in rows, but lie like irregular, honeycomb cells, separated by ridges sufficiently wide for a man to pass, and in some are signs of rough walling. It is remarkable that this old home should have remained thus undisturbed for so many genera-tions—say 2000 years? Probably the British boys played on the stones that lie about before ever the Romans were heard of by these islanders. Native oak and ash trees of considerable size grow on the place, some rooted into the founda-tions of the huts.

From here, passing the Delves again, we went through the gamekeeper's fold, up the bank by Snick gate, locally *Snek yat*, to Moor hill end, and across to the Egton bridge and Pickering road át Swinstey on the moor top, overlooking Goadland moor and the high grounds toward Whitby and Saltersgate, and the picturesque valley of the Murk Esk, with the railway from below Beck hole to the Incline top. The iron works at Beck hole were in operation; and we saw the line of the railway, up Eller beck, constructed to do away with the dangerous slope, for many years worked by a stationary engine. Randay mere, Julian park, Hazle head, Wheeldale moor, Stape, Raindale head and Newton, lie between here and Levisham station. The mere has been a deep lake, but is now a peat bog, having only a small pond at the upper end. Where the village of Julian park stands, a house in a Buck park stood. The dyke that fenced it in can be traced from the mere, round the moors, to the opposite side of the houses; and formerly Julian castle or fort, belonging to the de Mauleys of Mulgrave, stood below. The present tenant of the land told me that his father and he dug up the foundations, over half an acre, and brought the site into cultivation. We here, also, tread upon the Roman way that lead from Cawthorn camps to Dunsley wyke, a hard bit of stoning, which the farmer said he could not make a shallow grip through without using his pick. At Hazle head, again, is a distinct piece upon the green, hitherto untouched, though in most other places the road is destroyed.   Here are also clear springs of water just off the line of the Roman way and at the foot of the hill on Wheeldale beck, near "t'weather house garth," a hundred yards to right of the present highway, is a heap of slag called the "cinder hill," site of a Roman smelting place.   This fork of Wheeldale beck is very wild moorland.   On both sides of Mauley cross, a boundary stone on the moor seven miles from Egton bridge, the Roman way ran almost parallel to the present road.

Heather grows freely on all the moors, and the dales going from them into Newton dale are deep and narrow and full of trees.   There is a fine view from Newton bank into Newton dale, in which lies the railway, up to Raindale mill and the banks beyond, which close in the dale that way.   From this point, Levisham station, downward to Pickering the railway passes for six miles between steep banks covered by trees, disclosing beautiful views as it winds along Pickering beck.   If the line were now to be made it would probably be laid down straighter. Being originally a horse track there was less need to avoid sharp curves.

Three days may be well spent in this walk. Stokesley, Castleton and Egton bridge have good inns.

II.

WESTERN SLOPES OF THE CLEVELAND HILLS AND THE HAMBLETONS.

Arncliffe—" House of Mount Grace of Ingleby"—Osmo-
therly — A "mountaneous country" — Thimbleby—
Nether Silton—Kepwick—Kirkby Knowle—Westow
hall—Boltby Scar—Feliskirk—Mount St. John—Vale
of Mowbray—The Mowbrays.

PROFESSOR PHILLIPS says this
region "is one of the pleasantest
parts of Yorkshire, being in general
fertile, well-sheltered and woody,
with magnificent hills and mountains for the back
ground of rich domestic pictures." And so it is.
Delightful is the walk among its pretty villages
from Ingleby Arncliffe to Feliskirk and Thirsk,
through scenery ever varying—here woodlands;
there well tilled arable and meadow lands;
throughout a succession of green knolls, with
cattle grazing, and not unfrequently clumps of
trees on the tops. On the east, the Cleveland
hills and the Hambletons, from Arncliffe to
Rolston scar, ranging in height from over 800 to

near 1300 feet, break off at irregular distances
toward the west; and between and in advance
of their abrupt banks, for a space of three or
four miles in breadth, lie rounded hollows, and
slopes, more or less steep and long, declining
toward the great central vale of the county, with
hills and swelling grounds elevated from 100 to
700 feet above the general level of the vale;
while on the sides of, and among, the knolls and
hows rest farms and villages and pleasant mansions, making more attractive still these naturally
picturesque localities.

East Harsley, two miles from Welbury station,
standing on a mound 120 feet or so above the
Wisk, which rises near and flows northward, on
its remarkable course, just below, is a farm
village with a simple little church, a large hall
and the site of a "camp," probably Roman.
From it we see the tower of Mount Grace priory,
and farther on Eston beacon, Rosebury, Cook's
pillar, Cotcliff, and other points. At the foot of
the hills rests Arncliffe hall, seat of Mr. and Mrs.
Brown, the present representatives of the well-
known north-Yorkshire Mauleverers, whose
home and burial place this has been for many
generations. The family, according to Graves
and Ord, traces itself backward, in this name
and on this estate, to Edward the IV's days, and
through its ancestors, the Colvilles and
Ingelrams, or Ingrams, to the reign of Edward
I., at least. Behind the hall is the rough face of

Arncliffe, for the greater part planted with trees. From the sides and top of the cliff are seen the Vale of Cleveland; the hills between which the Tees flows; the narrow gap in the mountains down which the Swale comes; the broad Wensleydale to Penhill and Adelbrough, and, eastward, the moors.

The ruins of the "House of Mount Grace of Ingleby" are situated close against Arncliffe bank, and cover a large space. This priory was founded, as is said, in 1396 by Thomas de Holland, Duke of Surrey, for a prior and monks of the order of Carthusians, and is described as a "unique specimen of a Carthusian house in Yorkshire," and as one of nine established in England. Many parts of the outer walls with other portions of the structure yet stand, though a good deal broken. Around the large square on the north, about seventy yards across, now grass, are said to have been twenty cells, the doorways and narrow, zigzag, openings into which are still seen in the walls. The church stood next on the south, in shape a cross. The tower and walls of the nave and transept, with part of the north wall of the choir still remain, and the foundations of the rest, as well as of many other adjacent buildings, are yet visible. South of the church is another inclosure, in and about which have been other buildings. Westward, through the old entrance gateway, is a large farm house adapted, it is said, out of the priory buildings for

a mansion house, by the Lascelles family, who
bought the priory estate in 1653 from the Hon.
Conyers Darcy, the then owner, and who sold it
to Timothy Mauleverer Esquire in 1744. The
date 1654, and initials T.L. are over the house
door. Within the wood, behind the ruins, is St.
John's well ; and half a mile up the cliff is a little
ruin called the Lady's Chapel, which is described
as the place where the monks of the priory were
buried. Some people of good name were
interred at the priory church, and chief among
these was the noble founder, whose bones are
stated to have been brought here from
Cirencester for burial. Leaving the chapel we
soon came in sight of "black Hambleton" and
then dropt down upon Osmotherley, a little town
in the hills kept together by linen weaving and
bleaching, having a church, a Friends' chapel
and a Wesleyan, two or three inns and the shaft of
an old market cross, with a large, and apparently
ancient, stone table close by it, but no market
now I believe. From the north, the town seems
in a hole, but from the south is seen to lie on a
hill side. Up the eastward hollow are indica-
tions of bold moorland scenery. We were pleased
with all this and told a native so, but he said
" Oh, this country's nowt for mountaneous
scenery till yeh get up a 'Amleton ; no sike a spot
i' all Yorkshire. It's a mountaneous country all
t'way to t'seea ; all 'ills an mowers an valleys."

Crossing Cod beck, which, ten miles lower

down, flows through Thirsk; and passing
Thimbleby and through the larch plantation of
Thimbleby bank, we see below us the village of
Over Silton and, on our left, the really *black*
Hambleton, with Arden moor on the same level,
and the great hollows that sweep round to the
cliffs above Kepwick about three miles forward.
We again looked to the vales of our three
northernmost rivers and saw, though not distinctly enough to name them, the long lines of
hills that stand about their sources, suffused with
the light of the setting sun. The next village,
Nether Silton, is distinguished by a very fair
country inn, the Golden Cup, and we stayed the
night there.

The footway from Nether Silton leads over a
blithe little stream with the dolorous name of
Sorrow beck, through meadows to Kepwick,
below which is a large limestone quarry having
its own railway. On the moor ends are ancient
tumuli and at the western extremity is a great
mound bearing the duplicate name " How-hill."
On the southern slope of these lie the village
and hall of Cowsby, overlooking a sort of large
cove in the moors, and facing the great hill called
Woolmoor, a name derived, as Mr. Grainge, in
his *Vale of Mowbray*, explains from *ulloh* and
mote—Woolmote or mart. We walk between
Woolmoor and the higher banks to Kirkby
Knowle, or Kirkby-under-knoll, the knoll being
a large mound capped with trees and named

"Knowle-hill." A picturesque gap separates this from the moors, and on the southern slope of the ridge just out of a wood, lies Westow, or Raventhorpe, hall, and lower down Boltby village. We went down the slope over Lunshaw beck, then up the opposite bank by Hesketh grange to the top of Boltby scar, where is a remarkable horse-shoe-shaped intrenchment, with ditch and mound very distinct, opening on to the edge of the cliff, and within and about it are large tumuli. Forward, we have nearly the same views as from Rolston scar and Whitstone cliff; whilst, backward, the moors, the terrace and temples over Rievaulx abbey are seen, and Easterside moor appears on the north-east. From several points we see the knoll where stands the mansion called New Building, formerly said to have been Kirkby Knowle castle, which appears in the trees south of Woolmoor and which has a long history. It belonged to the now late Mr. C. H. Elsley, as also did Kirkby Knowle with other property, Whitstone cliff included. Mr. Elsley built nice schools at Kirkby and Feliskirk, and the natives are puzzled to make out the old-shaped letters of his motto and to tell whether the five roses on his shield are roses or tortoises; they think the latter.

From Boltby scar we went by the mill on Gurtof beck to Feliskirk, a pretty village at the foot of Mount St. John, having an interesting church, lately repaired, cross-shaped with a curved east end, in early days belonging, with lands here and elsewhere, to the Knights Hospitallers of St. John of Jerusalem, from whose Preceptory on the hill comes the name Mount St. John. The mansion has been rebuilt, and some of the Knights' lands are held by the Archbishopric of York. Feliskirk is about three miles from Thirsk.

The several villages in our walk are so separated by hills and woods that scarcely one can be seen from another; and, from the configuration of the ground, they lie much farther apart than would appear by the map. The country which lies south of the Cleveland boundary, between Mount Grace and Arncliffe hall, is part of the "Vale of Mowbray," itself a portion of the great Vale of York, five or six miles broad by twenty long, reaching to Hovingham. The names of the powerful Mowbrays frequently occur in all the local histories, as in the national; and, numerous as the noteworthy men of this family were, none is more prominent than the crusading Roger, who appears to have come of age and into possession of his lands about 1140 and who is said to have died a monk in his own abbey of Byland, one of thirty-five religious houses which he is described to have founded, though Mr. Ingledew remarks that Hoveden says he died in the Holy Land. A great deal may be read of him and his ancestors and successors, and the events they were concerned with, in Mr. Grainge's book, which contains precise histories of Thirsk and the places round about it. Also in Gill's *Vallis Eboracensis*; Ingledew's *North Allerton*, and elsewhere.

The "Tontine" inn near Mount Grace no longer exists, but the "Blue Bell" is still hung out at Ingleby Cross. Osmotherley and Nether Silton have comfortable inns, and some at Thirsk are excellent. We spent two days in this short walk.

III.

BILSDALE AND RYEDALE ; AND FROM HELMSLEY
ACROSS THE HAMBLETONS TO THIRSK.

"Stowsleh"—Clay hill—Bilsdale—The Rye—Scenery—
Rievaulx abbey—The Terrace — Duncombe park —
Helmsley, castle, church — The Hambletons, hotel,
views from Rolston scar—"T'wite 'orse an t'wite mare"
—Gormire.

COMING from Stokesley, by some called *Stowsleh* (*ow* as in now) southward through the long village of Broughton to the Cleveland hills, we face Cringley moor and Cold moor end, in the local dialect *Creenay* and *Caudmer*, to left of which, against Hasty bank, stand the tall Wain stones—called *wean* or *wearn*—seen both here and on the opposite side in Bilsdale. "Caudmer end's a rig at gangs doon into Bilsdil, and t'roond 'ill to west is Oleton 'ill and if iver t'clood cloases in 'tween t'ill and bank we get it 'ere." So said a road mender who had "bin 'ere an at Bilsdil 'eead aboon fifty year." On our way by Clay hill round Hasty bank to Bilsdale head, we have magnificent views of Easby moor, Rosebury, Eston beacon and the Vale of Cleveland, with the country up to and beyond the smoking towns of Darlington, Stockton and Middlesbrough. The wild plants grow luxuriantly along this bank, the roses and honeysuckles being perfect, the hazles full of nuts, and the wild strawberries bearing their small, sweet fruit.

Bilsdale head is shut in by high moors, and here begins the beck which flows through the dale till it meets the Rye near Shaken bridge, whence the augmented stream passes downward by Rievaulx abbey, Duncombe park, and Helmsley town, into the Vale of Pickering ; and then, after receiving the waters of half a dozen other becks and small rivers, runs into the Derwent, sixteen miles below Helmsley and twice that distance from Bilsdale head. Several other feeders of the Derwent are long streams, but this stream, running across nearly the whole length of the Cleveland hills and the Hambletons, called by its several names of Bilsdale beck, Seph and Rye is the longest. The scenery from Bilsdale and Ryedale is bold and extensive. The moors rise in many cases 600 or 700, or more, feet above the valley, are often picturesque in form and grouping, and have an abundance of trees. The low grounds seem about equally divided into arable and grass and have a fair quantity of live stock in them. When we past down, the dale was delightfully scented with the new hay. At Bilsdale head the farmers were just beginning the hay harvest; lower down they were almost ready for "leading." All Bilsdale is out of Cleveland, the southern boundary of that district being near Bilsdale head, two miles east of which is Burton head, the highest part, as before mentioned, of the north-eastern moors. There appears to be no village called Bilsdale, but many pleasant collections of houses exist in the dale, such as Seave green and Chop gate—*yat*. The latter, eight miles from Stokesley, has a fair inn.

We went upon Nab end opposite Orterley to see the bridestones, "supposed druidical," a circle of stones near one large pile, here called a *rook*, a contracted form of *currick, curig, careg* or *craig* (?) and near which the farmers have set up many smaller rooks. The moors are wild to the east, but about the Hag house farmstead, in the deep valley at the junction of Tripsdale and Tarn hole becks, the nabs grow plenty of wood, as also do the sides of Ledge beck down to Bilsdale again. A Ledge beck farmer told us that "just up i' that gill is tarn 'ole at goes into t'stanes where t'foxis goes into yearth, an' reight up at moor ist' stanes call'd watter stanes, quite, as yan may say, comical places 'ere. All Bilsdel's Lord Feversham's except Leng's at Chop yat and a little bit more of a man's at keeps two kye; I forget wheeah hes't noo." We turned off the high road and past Broadway foot, or Wain head, to Shaken bridge where the Rye, coming out of the hills, joins the Seph. Looking up the Rye, we have fine scenes of heights more or less clothed with trees, and long green banks going down into intersecting valleys. The bold moor Easterside, seen from other points, stands on the right; behind is a steep bank covered with trees, and below us, the two streams passing down to the bridge. As the farmer's wife said "it's a sweet ro-mantic place." We followed the stream to Rievaulx abbey, between woods, and slopes now covered with green crops but soon, in many places, to become golden with ripe corn. The ruins of the abbey rest between the hills a little above the stream, overlooking the few acres of grass land which separate the steep banks of the river. Rievaulx strikes us at first as not unlike Bolton in its accessories of wood and water and green fields. Something peculiar is expected in such a site ; and, indeed, without some special fitness this ground would probably not have been chosen for the sacred edifice ; but it is unpleasantly different from Bolton in having a village of poor cottages built, not only upon foundations of walls that are down, but close against those that are standing, and con- structed also with the stones of the abbey itself. The ruins in fact have been treated as a con- venient quarry. We see the old masons' marks on the walls of the houses all round ; the village corn mill is ornamented with a row of six carved stone corbels, sticking out of the front in a meaningless way, and the blacksmith's shop has similar adornments. And yet many years ago the fine terrace of close shaven grass, twenty or thirty yards wide and half a mile long, was formed to overlook the ruins and the valley wherein they lie; and the two "temples" at the ends, one with pillared front and elaborately painted ceiling (Italian painter at work they say seven years at a guinea a day) and the other round, and floored with tessalated pavement from the abbey, were built for the same purpose. We see from the terrace a great stretch of wood, valley and moor land, north, south and west. The abbey with its dependent structures has covered much ground. As a man said, "there are acres of walls." The ruins now standing are chiefly those of the church and refectory. The choir of the church stands nearly north and south. Some walls are in excellent condition and there is stone work that looks like new, and the upper windows of the choir in particular are richly ornamented. The arches are rounded in some places, but generally pointed—"transition from Norman to the early pointed style of architecture." Almost within the abbey walls is a large heap of old slag from iron smelting, now used for road material, and half a mile down the valley, about a house called the Forge, other heaps, all believed to be the refuse of iron smeltings for the purposes of the abbey; but if the first be, it seems strange that the inmates should stack an ugly mound of black rubbish at the door of their beautiful house.

Duncombe park (Lord Feversham's) stands about two miles lower down in magnificent woods over the Rye.   People are allowed on weekdays to walk or drive through the park and see the house.   The mansion is supposed to have been designed by Sir John Vanburgh.   It was mainly built, as I read, in 1718, but the two wings and conservatory have been erected under Sir Charles Barry's superintendence.   The house is said to have splendid rooms, adorned with many valuable paintings and pieces of sculpture. We did not go into it, but walked along the close cut, grassy terraces, which are formed about it, a mile in length, upon the steep banks of the Rye, through ornamental plantations and shrubberies, where numerous evergreens and most of our native trees grow well.   We cannot see the Hambletons from the terraces, nor the Wolds, the latter being shut out by trees ; but there are splendid views of the moors east and north-east, and Ryedale itself with its alternate full grown woods and green slopes is exceedingly beautiful.

At the foot of, and just within, the park, stand the ruins of the once strong Helmsley castle pulled down by the Parliament after the siege of 1644.   This castle covered several acres of ground, had two moats and two entrance gates, one about seventeen yards inside the other, and a high keep with many subsidiary buildings. The arch of the outer gateway, the walls of the inner, part of the great tower, portions of the walls and of one or two side towers, and also a square building like a mansion-house, are still standing. The moats also remain; but now large trees, chiefly ash, grow about the ruins, shewing that many years have past since the fortress was dismantled. Mr. Gill in his *Vallis Eboracensis* says the castle was partially restored and became the favourite retreat of the Duke of Buckingham after he had retired from the court of Charles II.; and that the range of apartments constituting his mansion-house (the building just named) was probably built when the Villiers family succeeded to the property. The Rye flows past when there is surface water; in droughty weather all the stream is swallowed higher up, and the bed is dry. The park gates are on one side of the clean little town of Helmsley "blackamoor" which lies at the foot of several valleys. From the high ground north of the town we see many miles of the Howardian hills, and the wolds across the wide Vale of Pickering.

Helmsley has many old buildings; one or two are wooden-framed houses and others of this kind have been pulled down lately. The church has been patched up; the original high-pitched roofs of nave and porch have been lowered, and the present ugly porch hides a Norman doorway formerly resting on pillars, nearly all now broken out.

Leaving Helmsley again and crossing Rievaulx bridge, we have views of the abbey plain, and the terrace with its temples, and the woods down stream one way, and of Scawton hole, as they call the (in part) dry valley running up to the Hambletons, the other way; and passing Scawton village and the rickety barn called its church, we reach the moor top and the Hambleton hotel, where are stables for race horses, seven miles alike from Helmsley and from Thirsk. Several other dry valleys go down to Ryedale, and looking across these to the north over the villages of Cold Kirkby and Old Byland we see the bold moor Easterside, and Bilsdale, Arden, Rievaulx and Helmsley moors, while eastward the surfaces of the moors to those which border the sea coast, thirty miles off, are overlooked. The Hambletons grow a sort of short bent grass, heather and ling, with bilberry wires.

Coming to the top of the cliffs, we have magnificent views of the great Vale of York with its towns and villages south and west. Looking over Thirsk we see into Wensleydale, with Penhill, thirty miles off, overhanging it; left of that Harland hill and other bold mountain tops more distant, among which we make out the Nidd Whernsides. There was a haze which prevented us seeing further and also shut out York; but we are told that on clear days Mickle fell and neighboring hills, fifty miles distant, can be seen from Whitstone cliff. Nearer, and of

course more distinct, are the moors of Colster-
dale, Masham, Kirkby-malzeard, Dallowgill and
others, bounding the great vale on the west.
Immediately under us lie the picturesque hills
about Kirkby-knowle, Feliskirk, Oldstead,
Kilburn and Byland, amongst which Hood hill
in front of Rolston scar is very prominent.
Coxwold and Newburgh park, too, lie only a few
miles to the south in the narrow opening connecting the Vales of York and Pickering.   Just
below Whitstone cliff is Gormire, a small lake
covering about sixteen acres, and here, as in
Berkshire, we have a white horse, and a white
mare too.—" T' wite mare is under Wissuncliff
an' t' wite 'orse is just a back at' bank facin t'toon
o' Kilb'n.   T' wite 'orse wodn't shew itself aboon
as it wod below.   It's clean'd a' brack'ns ivery
year an chalk't oot.   Tommy Taylor at's gone
tuv Australia 'ed it pick't oot for a memorandum
not so very monny years sin ; may be ten years
mebbe.   Taylor wur born at Kilb'n an 'e got a
taumst'n put up for all t' family livin an' deead
an' put their names on; a particular sort of a
man.   Ther's none on 'em left noo.   Ther's
'unerds an' thoosans comes to Germire.   I'se
gawin that road in a minit."—And so we waited
for the Kilburn woman who told us this.   The
white horse is seen distinctly from the railway as
we approach Thirsk from York and also on the
Thirsk and Malton line.   Gormire, one of our
few Yorkshire lakes, is said to have been created

by a landslip, is surrounded by hills, fed by unseen springs, and has no outlet on the surface. The lower ground under the great cliffs consists of rounded and picturesque knolls for a mile or two and then falls off toward Thirsk. Rolston scar with Hood hill in front, Whitstone cliff and Boltby scar are prominent objects from the railways to York and Leeds.

Good entertainment may be had at Stokesley, Chop Gate, Helmsley, Hambleton hotel and Thirsk. This is a three or four days walk.

IV.

COXWOLD, BYLAND, KIRKDALE AND BRANSDALE, AND FARNDALE.

Newburgh priory; its owners; Lady Fauconberg; Cromwell—Coxwold; church; Shandy hall—Byland abbey—Wass—Duncombe park and Helmsley again—Etton and other gills—Kirkdale, cave, church, beck—Bransdale—Rudland rigg—Farndale—Obstrusch roque—Gillamoor—Hutton le hole—Appleton le moors; new church—Sinnington.

NEAR seven miles from Thirsk, on the undulating ground which lies about the junction of the Vales of York and Pickering, stands the pleasant little town of Coxwold; and within half a mile of it, Newburgh park, the seat of Sir George Orby Wombwell. The present mansion, which includes portions of the old monastic buildings of Newburgh priory, dating from 1145, one of the thirty-five religious houses founded by Roger de Mowbray, stands low; and that seemed to us its fault, for in other respects it is an agreeable residence. It has been for many generations in the hands of owners allied to each other in such

a way as to form almost one family, though the
names have changed ; and many portraits bearing these names—Belasyse, Fauconberg, Wombwell—as well as the names of personages
connected with them, hang in the rooms and
galleries.   Among others are one or two con-
temporary portraits of Lady Mary Fauconberg,
the Protector's daughter, who had a Cromwellian
face ; also a metal medalion of the head of
Oliver himself, into which the moulder has put
signs of care ; and a painting of George Villiers
Duke of Buckingham, wherein the hair is yellow
and the face not bad looking.   Here are other
memorials of Cromwell ; and some say his bones
were brought to Newburgh, when turned out of
their grave after the Restoration.   The house
contains tapestry and furniture and other signs
of an old occupation.   The park itself is
extensive and splendid trees grow in it.   I read
that the first Belasyse was chaplain to Henry
VIII.   Thomas Belasyse was made Baron
Fauconberg by Charles I.   He died in 1652 and
was buried at Coxwold.   The Wombwells are
the old family which is named from its former
home of Wombwell near Barnsley, and the
present Baronet is the third owner of his name.
In Coxwold church are monuments of the
Belasyses and Fauconbergs.   One, dated 1603,
is an extraordinary structure, built up piramidally
and full of pillars with capitals, cornices and
rows of shields, and, at the foot of it, in homely

character, the builder, who was probably the
designer also, has carved the following—

Thomas Browne Did Carve this Tome
Himself alone of Hesselwood Stone.

The church itself has a large south porch,
uniform windows, and an octagonal tower
without spire.   Inside, the ceiling panels are
whitened, and so are all the plain walls.   There
is no aisle.   This was Sterne's church and
Shandy hall where he lived stands at a short
distance on the north-west.   It is a two-gabled
house, close to the highway, and is now occupied
as three cottages.   The vicarage, and the
grammar school, founded in 1603 by Sir John
Harte, grocer, of London, are near the church.

In a hollow beneath the Hambletons, a mile
and a half north-east of Coxwold, we come to
the ruins of Byland abbey.   The buildings have
been very extensive.   The estate is now divided,
part being owned by Mr. Stapylton of Myton
and part by Ampleforth college, and the highway
cuts it into two.   West of the road are only an
arch or two, with pieces of walling, and some
foundations ; eastward stand the remains of the
church and other buildings.   The high and
beautiful western front, with the lower part of
the great round window thirty feet in diameter,
is prominent among these.   The walls of the
northern aisle, transept, and chancel of the
church, up to several courses above the window
openings, are also standing; and there are

E 2

many walls and foundations of walls on the south side. The window and door openings are all bevelled from about four feet to eight feet, or in that proportion according to size, and numerous details of windows, brackets, arches, and clustered shafts of pillars, are very pleasing. They shew a conformity with each other for general effect, and much variety in special designs and workmanship. The best side to see the extent of the ruined walls is the north-east. A quarter of a mile off is the improved village of Wass, which will become one of the nicest in the district if the owner goes on as he has begun.

We walked from here across the Rye by the mill and through Duncombe park to Helmsley again ; and, in the evening, up the pretty little valley called Etton gill, down which a beck comes to the Rye. Half a mile up it is filled with trees, and a mile further it forks into two, each fork having a beck. It is still full of trees upward ; and, as we came back after dark, we heard the strong voices of owls calling aloud their clear to-whoo. Many other dales, short and long between here and Pickering beck, stretch through the southern portion of the north eastern moors into the Vale of Pickering. Those we pass, going eastward from Helmsley, are Ashdale ; "Con howl," wooded, I believe, to the moor top ; Riccal dale, wooded for four or five miles ; and Goodam dale. We also go through the well-to-do united villages of Beadlam and

Nawton, where the soil is good but water scarce. Several places hereabout, obtain their water by means of narrow, artificial grips, cut for long distances and called "water races."

Between four and five miles from Helmsley we arrive at Kirkdale, locally *Keddil*, where the celebrated bone cave lies. The entrance to the cave is in the face of a limestone quarry, fourteen or fifteen feet above the present floor, but double that above the stream. Within a few score yards of this stands the also well known, ancient little church of Kirkdale, remote and silent, lying in a pretty hollow among trees and away from any dwelling-house. The quietude was impressive. No sound of the beck was heard, for the water sinks half a mile above and the bed was dry; not a soul came there but ourselves while we stayed, nor any other living being save birds; and it did one good to spend a solemn half hour in the simple church yard. Within the unpretentious porch of the most westerly of the two south doors, above the round arch of the doorway, we read the remarkable inscription discovered in late times (1771 Dr. Young says) recording that *Orm, Gamal's son, bought Saint Gregory's church when it was all broken and fallen; and that he it made new from the ground to Christ and Saint Gregory in the days of Edward the King and in the days of Tosti the Earl*—a date which Dr. Young shews to have been not later than the year 1064. Though this inscription has been described in several books I may be pardoned for reprinting it. The central portion represents a rude sun dial, and the words at the top and in the half circle say, *This is day's sun mark at every tide* [*hour*]; and those at the bottom are, *and Hawarth me wrought and Brand the Presbyter*. The stone is over seven feet long and nearly two feet broad, and the letters and lines are now blacked. The church walls appear as if rebuilt long after the date of the inscription; but Dr. Young says this stone and the Saxon door beneath it have remained undisturbed. A small portion of a Saxon inscription, with a sun dial, was also found at the church of Edstone on the hill two miles south of this. The plain, square tower of Kirkdale

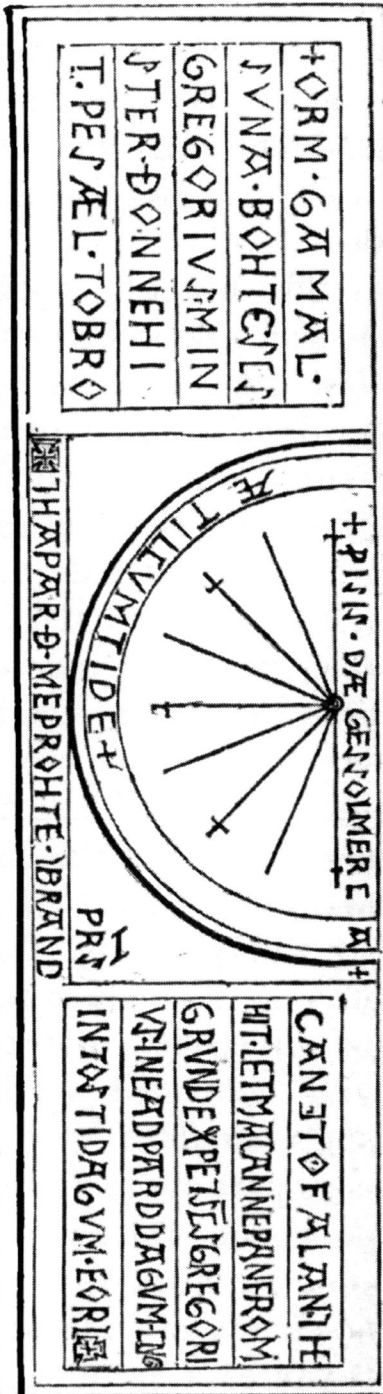

church is modern, and new stone appears
in part of the chancel. The body of the church
is older, and so is the eastern end of the chancel,
with its three, long, thin lights; and in some
places ancient memorial stones are inserted in
the walls.

From this beautiful spot we went through
greenest fields, between rich woods, up the dale
by the winding beck. As before mentioned, the
bed was dry for some distance. Above the
"sink" there was a good flow of water. The
stream bears the name of Hodge beck, but the
several parts of the dale have different names,
as Kirkdale, Skiplam dale, Sleightholm dale and
Bransdale, locally *Brancedil.* In that respect,
as well as in general character, this dale and
Ryedale and Farndale are alike. For the first
four miles above Kirkdale there are rich, wood-
land views; and then the valley widens, and has
farms and more cultivated lands. There is no
regular highway through Bransdale. Eight or
nine miles up, the dale is narrow in the bottom
and much diversified, all the lower slopes having
trees and cultivated fields; and hereabout,
extending a length of two or three miles, we find
the greater part of the population. Standing on
the high ground, north of High Lidmoor house,
we overlook a broad space, set with farm buildings and clumps of trees, and with cattle grazing
in the pastures. Farndale, which, as just mentioned, is very like Bransdale, lies parallel to the

latter at about three miles distance.   It is
picturesque near the Low mill where Horn end
comes down ; and from the moor above it, called
Rudland rigg, we see the sites of Cawthorne camps
and Cropton, the church spires of Appleton le
moors and Pickering ; the moors toward the sea
coast, and the wolds.

About a mile west of the low mill lies the
haunted circle called " Obtrusch Roque," a
double ring of stones placed in the ground, with
remains of a stone chest in the centre.   The
inner circle is about seven yards in diameter ; and
the stones of the outer stand six or seven yards
from those of the first.   The flag stones which
composed the chest have been let down by
digging, and those who displaced them have not
put them right again.   A great quantity of loose
stones, removed from the surface of the moor,
almost covers the rings.   When Professor
Phillips saw the place, as described in his *Rivers
&c. of Yorkshire, p.* 210, it was a mound covered
with heath.   He and his friends removed the
collection of stones and found each of the two
circles consist of twenty-five or twenty-six stones
on edge, and the sides of the kist composed of
four flag stones, set edgeways, pointing east,
west, north and south, the greatest length being
from east to west.   They did not find urn, bone
or treasure ; but the countrymen said this place
of ancient burial had been opened many years
before and then gold had been found in it ; and

he concludes—"considering the position of the kist, set with careful attention to the cardinal points; the two circles of stone; the number of these stones, which, if completed, appeared to be 26; it seemed no unreasonable conjecture that the construction contained traces of astronomical knowledge, of the solar year, and weekly periods. I dare not confidently affirm this. Was this a relique of an early British chief or of a later Scandinavian warrior? for such circles have been raised in Scandinavia and the Orkney Islands by the Northmen, and this is a district which the Northmen colonized. A similar circle of stones occurs at Cloughton near Scarborough."

The view down Farndale as we walk from Obtrusch with the farms, plantations, and uneven surface, and the high banks near Gillamore, where the valley contracts, is very fine. From the latter point to Keldholm the dale is narrower; and then it opens into the Vale of Pickering. Obtrusch stands about six miles from Kirkby Moorside and four from Gillamore. East of the latter is Hutton le hole; and from Hutton common there are picturesque views up Farndale, through which dale flows the little river Dove.

We walked from Kirkby Moorside through Hutton and Appleton le moors to Sinnington, or Sevenington, so called from the name of its river; and thence by Wrelton, Aislaby and

Middleton to Pickering. · At Appleton the lady of the hall is erecting a little church, which in many of the details is very interesting, and frequently excellent, though often too heavy for the size of the structure. The spire is quadrangular and ornamented ; and the round west window and deeply sunk doorway have a good effect. Many modern decorations and materials are employed within ; but we thought the roof far too plain for so elaborate a building, and there was a want of light in the church. We found nothing more to interest us in our walk except the rural village of Sinnington, where is an old, ruined, chapel, which has some good window openings and is now used as a barn.

Coxwold, Byland, Helmsley, Kirkby Moorside and Pickering have inns. So have several of the villages, but I do not know of what sort. Four days ought to be allowed for this walk.

V.

MIDDLESBROUGH, GUISBROUGH, DANBY MOOR, EGTON BRIDGE. GLAISDALE, ROSEDALE, KIRKBY MOORSIDE TO HOVINGHAM.

Middlesbrough — Guisbrough, Priory, Alum works — Iron mines—Spa—Freebrough—British settlement on Danby Moor—The Beacon—Moors and Dales—Eskdale —Glaisdale End iron works—Egton Bridge again— Glaisdale—Rough Moors—Rosedale; Iron roasting; high level railway; Abbey ruins — Cropton — The Scoresbys—Appleton again—Keldholm priory—Kirkby Moorside—Nunnington—Cauklass Bank — Hovingham.

UPON the line of railway between South Stockton and Guisbrough lies the rapidly extending Middles brough, a place which has been made into a town within the last thirty-five years or less. In 1801 the census returns give the number of inhabitants as 25; in 1831 as 154; in 1851 as 7631; in 1861 as 18,992. In 1821 the compilers of Baines's directory did not find there any resident of sufficient importance as tradesman or farmer, to be named. In 1865 it was a corporate borough with a mayor, town clerk, and like officers, and near 30,000 inhabitants; and withal notable for an open and generous disposition, and the apparent consciousness, characteristic of the young and strong and hopeful, of unlimited powers of growth and progression. I have no doubt, any more than the burgesses have, that we shall some day read able speeches, delivered in the House of Commons by the member for Middlesbrough, who will refer to the fact of the quick rise of his borough with as much pride as English people usually do to that which is venerable for its old standing; and the house will sympathise with him, for in our happy nation we are proud of both present and past. Coal and railways, and facility of access by the Tees estuary have had a good deal of influence in developing the town, but the most efficient agent is the ironstone of the Cleveland hills.

After leaving Middlesbrough we enter a pretty country between the latter hills, the northerly faces of which appear in succession as we go on. We come to the well wooded lands of Ormesby; to Nunthorpe encircled with knolls, where Rosebury appears directly in advance of us; and, turning round the ends of Pinchinthorp and High cliff, come in sight of Guisbrough, which lies in a pleasant situation among the hills. The prominent objects as we approach are the priory ruins and the church. The beautiful

eastern gable of the priory church, contains
the window openings of the aisle and the
high and elegant arch of the great window,
which, being now open from the ground, is above
seventy feet high. This and a few bits of wall,
an arch and some coffins and loose stones,
constitute all that is left of the richly endowed
and magnificent structures of Guisbrough priory,
or at least all now to be found upon the site.
The priory is stated to have been founded by a
Bruce in 1119 and to have had enormous·
possessions in land. The grounds on which the
buildings stood belong to the Chaloner family,
and have so belonged for the last 300 years.
Mr. Ord points out, with sorrow and indignation,
that stones from the ancient buildings are to be
found in every quarter of the town and neighbourhood, broken pillars and pedestals being
converted into gate posts, and stands for water
casks, and even turned to worse uses. Men
employed by Captain Chaloner of Long Hull, the
present owner, were clearing the rubbish from
the foot of the great window and putting the
surface of the land into good order when I was
there.

About a mile to the eastward of the town lie
the places where the Alum house and works
belonging to the Chaloners were. Mr. Young
says Sir Thomas Chaloner began these about the
year 1600. They were discontinued some years
ago. The old story of the obtaining one of the

Pope's alum makers from Italy in a cask, by Sir Thomas, may still be heard at Guisbrough, though Mr. Ord discredits the notion of Italian workmen, and, quoting Fuller's Worthies, shows that the men came from Rochelle in France; and he gives, moreover, a portrait of one of these, Lambert Russell, who was a man of sufficient standing to wear a sword. Mr. Ord says that the extensive alum works of the Chaloners', which were at Belman bank, are universally acknowledged to be the oldest in this county. Iron mines are now worked on the same estate, and one of the mineral railways of Cleveland passes through it, and there seems to be great activity about the mines.

In a glen near to Slape Wath lies the once esteemed, but now deserted, Guisbrough Spa. The iron mines are close upon it and, before long, the dilapidated Spa houses will probably be buried under the refuse. The highway goes on from Slape Wath to Aysdale gate, and, ascending to the top of Stanghow moor, leads to Moorsholm moor, upon which stands Freebrough —locally *Freebreh*. The places just named lie six or seven miles from the coast, and the sea is visible from all the higher parts of the moors. Freebrough is an isolated hill, covering six or seven acres of ground, 821 feet above the sea or, according to my judgment, about 300 feet from the level of the moor. It is very like Blakey Topping, but more uniformly round, and it rises from flatter land. It is a hill of even slope on all sides, save as to a hollow place on the east, which, at a little distance, does not detract from the apparent roundness. Mr. Ord says this hollow was made in quarrying stone. We see from the summit depressions in the sea cliffs, such as Saltburn and Skiningrave, and a great extent of moors, beginning, at the time of this walk, to show patches of purple here and there, and Danby beacon howe was very distinct.

Taking note of landmarks I struck over the moors for the ancient British settlement, lying a mile north of the beacon hill, on a ridge between two feeders of the Staithes beck, the water in one of which is fit for drinking. I found the site of the old village very desolate. The ling about many of the pits had been lately burnt off, and most of the holes were full of sphagnum, sign of a generally damp situation. The plan of this village differs much from that of the settlement at Egton grange. There the huts stood almost close together and not in regular .order ; here the pits are in parallel lines, two rows being inclosed within banks of earth. The pairs of rows are three in number, each containing thirty or more houses, or about fifteen in a row. The pits measure about ten feet in diameter, and lie from fifteen to eighteen feet apart. The passage, or street, between the lines is about twenty four feet wide and the inclosing ridges lie almost close to the outsides of the rows. There are several plain upright stones on the moor about the pits, at considerable distances from each other, and many tumuli. Four of the latter are of great size, and three of these stand in a line a hundred yards apart and two or three hundred yards from the pits. I think the village at Egton grange occupied a site preferable to this.

Both from the northern side of Danby low moor, and from the Danby beacon howe, we have good views. From the stones of the demolished beacon we see the Durham coast over Up-Leatham hill; the new buildings at Saltburn-by-the-sea, and the open sea there, as well as beyond the south eastern cliffs, except where such high points as Huntcliff and Rock-cliff intervene. On the other hand are Easby moor; parts of Sleddale and Kildale; the moors south of these; the southern side of the Esk valley; the western sides of Wester and Danby dales with Castleton; then the dales of Little and Great Fryop, looking from this height as if one valley, shaped like a horse shoe with an elevated middle portion; and next, the eastern side of Glaisdale. The day was especially fine and warm, and a sweet scent of flowers came up with the west wind out of the dales on to the moor top. I walked by Lealholm side and along the Esk to Egton bridge, thus passing the wooded glens and steep banks of this part of the valley. From Glaisdale end to Grosmont, the North Yorkshire and Cleveland railway goes with the Esk through the narrow glen between Limber-hill and Arncliffe, crossing the water several times. The great ironworks at Glaisdale end will materially alter the appearance of that fine hollow.

I left Egton bridge early next morning. The lanes were sweet with honeysuckles and roses, and the walk through Arncliffe wood to the foot of Snowden nab was very cool and pleasant. Glaisdale is broad and uneven toward the end. The bottoms are dotted over with trees, and the gulleys, where water flows, are marked out by thick foliage. One of the best views is just south of the Methodist chapel, where the dale head appears circular, and whence the more southerly farms, with their clumps of trees and fields divided by hedge rows, are all seen at once. From the dale head all the valley is in sight, appearing the same sort of dale as the Fryops. It is a hard walk of three miles across the rough moor from Glaisdale head to Rosedale head and not interesting.

Rosedale is a long dale, very busy now, in the upper part, with railroad making, stone quarry-ing, ironstone mining and the building of furnaces to "roast" the iron in. On the moor top, half a mile south west of Rosedale village stands the well known chimney, seen on all sides for many miles round ; and the high level mineral railway goes to it from Stockton and Middlesbrough. There is much arable land in this dale. At the

village, which stands pleasantly, are the remains
of the ancient abbey, described by Dr. Young
and other authorities as founded as early as
1190 by a de Stuteville, one of the family which
owned Stuteville castle near Kirkby Moorside.
Most of the walls which would have attracted
attention as belonging to an abbey are pulled
down. The lower part of a staircase with two
door openings, one over the other ; a bit of wall
with the pillars of one side of a doorway ; a few
memorial slabs ; two stones like heads of stalls ;
a simple stone chair and a few other things are
the only peculiar remains I saw. One tomb
stone, standing on its head, appears to be that
of *Sister Catherine Meger* described by Dr.
Young. The letters ...RINA and ...ER were all
I made out up-side down. The ancient lintel,
with " Omnia Vanitas " in Saxon characters, is
now built into the wall over the door of the
present very plain chapel. Near these ruins are
buildings which have either belonged to the
abbey or been built with stones taken from it.
Dr. Young describes the square, south of the
ruins, as the square of the abbey cloisters.
There are two good inns here, and both keep
post horses. The village is ten miles from
Pickering. It appears that the existence of
ironstone in this locality has been long known.
A forge is said to have been in operation near
the abbey in the early part of Edward III.'s
reign, and the remains of old smelting works are

found on the moor side three miles down the dale.

Five miles from the abbey is the village of Cropton, birth place of the Yorkshire farmer-boy, afterward Captain William Scoresby the elder. The situation of Cropton is remarkable. It stands upon a steep hill, which, from the valley, looks like a great howe, and the road up to it passes between that and another equally bold prominence. These are on the ridge that stretches from Newton dale to Rosedale, in the middle of which lie the Cawthorn camps about two miles from Cropton. We see Rawcliff and the situation of the camps as we approach Cropton. From the high grounds the long Rosedale is seen; and very beautiful it is in the lower part, being well wooded and green. The stream—the Seven—flows by Cropton mill down the valley, toward Sinnington, between deep and well wooded banks. The church at Cropton, which is new, stands near a circular mound, called Hallgarth hill, about which are trenches and ridges indicating the site of buildings. I believe none of the Scoresbys resides here now. People know the captain was born at Nutholm in Cropton; and his father, also a William, who died at Wrelton in August 1816 in his 84th year, was buried in Cropton church yard. The captain died 28 April 1829, and was buried in Whitby church yard. Doctor Scoresby, the third William, died at Torquay 21 March 1857, and was interred at Upton church.

F 2

Coming down the hill again, I struck off into the perfumed lanes across the stream at Cropton mill ; then up the bank into Birkhead wood, and by Appleton le moors, through the fields to Kirkby Moorside, anciently, they say, Moors*head*. The footway takes us through a splendid, agricultural country, overlooking a great plain, marked out by trees and bounded by hills south, west, and north. The opening up the little river Dove, as we go down toward it, is very nice ; and just below us, in a pretty spot, is the site of Keldholm priory—a nunnery I believe—founded by a de Stuteville, a relative of the founder of Rosedale abbey. Only the site and a few stones remain, though the modern house is called the Priory. Half a mile farther, up the hill, stands Kirkby Moorside. On the east of the town was the castle of the de Stuteville family. Nothing remains but the site from which there is a noble prospect over the wide vale of Pickering. Another castle, or hall, at the north end of Castle-gate, belonged to the Neviles, and the present Tolbooth was erected out of it. The house in which the Duke of Buckingham died is still to be seen, at the corner of Tinley-garth street. The land, southward from Kirkby Moorside, is flat for five or six miles, and then we come to a narrow range of heights prolonged from the Hambletons. Nunnington lies on one side of it, and Stonegrave on the other. The highway goes up the Nunnington slope through an avenue

of old trees, half a mile long ; and from the top
of Cauklass bank, which is the name of the
declivity looking south, we have a grand view of
the Hambletons above Oswaldkirk ; of the moors
northward to the Cleveland hills, and of those
that stretch eastward beyond Pickering; and
also of the hills and woods of the Castle Howard
range, with the towns of Hovingham and Gilling
at the foot; and, beyond these, of the wolds.
Hovingham is about nine miles from Kirkby
Moorside. As we go by railway to Thirsk we
pass the White horse, Rolston scar, and Hood
hill ; and see Whitstone cliff, Boltby scar and
others of the Hambletons.

Places of inns — Stockton, Middlesbrough,
Guisbrough, Egton bridge, Rosedale, Kirkby
Moorside—all good. Three days or more may
be pleasantly spent between Stockton and
Hovingham.

VI.

ON THE SEA CLIFFS OF CLEVELAND, OR REDCAR TO WHITBY.

Iron furnaces—Redcar—Saltburn — Huntcliff — Lofty Rockcliff—Skiningrave — Edges of Cliffs— Romantic Staithes, Capt. Cook, fishermen, herring season and N.E. winds—Rosedale Wyke — Hinderwell — Runswick; houses on ledges—Slippery Claymoor bank—The blue sea—Lyth—Mulgrave park—Sandsend—Dunsley bay and Whitby strand,

VERY striking is the appearance of the iron-smelting country on the Tees, as we travel by railway after dark to Redcar, when the glare of successive furnaces accompanied by clouds of smoke alternates with the gloom that comes in between. Works are now set up within about four miles of Redcar, but the residents there say the long streams of smoke do not reach them. Redcar, with Coatham, is growing larger along the sandy shore. It had a little over 400 people fifty years ago and above 1500 in 1861. It has now more. In the last week of August, 1864, as calculated

from the "Gazette," there were, in the 250
lodging houses and inns of the two places, above
1000 visitors, chiefly from Durham and Yorkshire, a good many out of the West-riding.
Redcar has few fishermen, having only eight or
ten cobles carrying three men a piece. They
now live in better dwellings than the unhealthy
square that stood above the beach a few years
ago. Coatham has, among other good things, a
modern church "in the early decorated style of
architecture," with spire forming a prominent
figure in the landscape; and Mr. Tweddell calls it
"decidedly the most beautiful church in Cleveland." There is a great breadth of sand at
Redcar and along the shore past Marske, two
miles east, to Saltburn, five miles east; and at
low water the hard lias scars, that begin half a
mile from shore and are at least that space long
and broad, are left bare. About six miles off,
across the estuary, lies the flat, sea-side village,
Seaton-carew, fashionable generations back, but
which ceased to be so long since; and beyond
that Hartlepool, which Mr. Ord dignifies by the
name "Venice of the North."

The railway now reaches "Saltburn-by-the
sea," a new place so called to distinguish it from
the little old village of two or three houses, lying
just below in a hole near the level of the sea
shore. At the rising town, which stands about
150 feet above the sands that stretch along [the
beach, and which has fine views of land and sea,

is the large, well built, and grand-looking Zetland
hotel, opened in 1863 I believe, at a cost of
between £30,000 and £40,000, occupying the
top of the cliff over the deep glen, down which
the burn comes to the sea from the woody hollows below Skelton and the slope of Upleatham.
The coast was very attractive on the particular
morning of our walk for we had a sunny sky and
a rough sea, the north-east wind blowing up
white spray from the crests of the waves. Saltburn contains excellent houses beside the hotel,
and the style of building is good. We found in
1864 above twenty lodging houses and about
150 visitors. I hear the dwellings have much
increased since. Mr. Bell was then erecting, of
ironstone, a private mansion of striking appearance, looking seaward, half a mile up the glen.
This has been completed lately. The western
bank of the stream is laid out in pleasant paths
and Lord Zetland permits people to go through
the woods, which fill the little valley and stretch
backward from Saltburn to Skelton castle and Up-
leatham. Many will be glad to learn that the
noble exterior and fine rooms of the hotel are
worthily complemented with what, to English no-
tions, is more important: excellent provision for the
comfort of guests. A competent judge tells me
it has one of the best of cooks, and that the
cellar is superb! But Saltburn, for other reasons,
also, deserves to be one of our chief seaside
residences. Among these are a wide sea pros-

pect; proximity to some of the best scenery of
the coast-district, where we may face the bracing
air of the heights, or shelter ourselves in the
glens; good sea bathing; a firm belt of dry
sands, and facility of access by railway. I find
it commended for suitable drinking water, and
for a spring of mineral water, "like in flavour
and not much unlike in chemical constitution"
the Harrogate chalybeates of Tewitt's and St.
John's wells, with properties calculated to im-
prove debilitated persons and to agree with those
who use it. More than I have space for might
be said of the glories of this and all our other
watering places from Redcar to Filey. The
local books would form a library by themselves.
In those that relate to Redcar, Saltburn, and
Staithes, stirring tales may be read of the, now
happily ended, times when physical-force smug-
glers ran kegs of untaxed spirit and packages of
unentered goods into the small wykes of this
rugged coast, and stored them in holes in the
scars and steep hill sides, or in hidden cellars
under dwellings. But now

No fire-flash shines from the towering cliff,
No answering light burns blue in the skiff,
    No more they stand
    That smuggling band,
Some in the water, and some on the sand,
Ready their contraband goods to land;
Though nights are dark—*they* are silent and still;
There's no party to head; no Smuggler Bill!

       See 2 Ingoldsby Legends, 150.

We walked from Saltburn, under the shady trees, to the picturesque gorge in the shale above Marske mill, a mile from the shore; then turned toward Skelton, and round to old Saltburn, and ascended Huntcliff, crossing the mineral railway that winds about the hills, and having sight of the ocean and of the sands from Saltburn to Redcar, and the low-lying Hartlepools in the distance.   Inland our old acquaintance the evergreen Rosebury, with Ayton moor, and the round topped Freebrough showed themselves among adjacent heights.

The sea cliffs rise at Saltburn, and on Huntcliff, which is the bold mass we see from Redcar, attain a height, according to Prof. Phillips, of 360 feet, the beacon hill, a fourth of a mile back, being 549 feet; but four miles south east rises the "loftiest of all the precipices that guard the English Coast," the great Rockcliff, or Boulby cliff, which stands 666 feet above the sea.   From Huntcliff to Skiningrave tortuous footways conduct us over wasting sea cliffs, some cut down to mere gables of soft soil and destined soon to fall under the influence of sea and wind.   Skiningrave was anciently *Skengrave* or *Skengrif*, grif meaning a narrow rough valley or chasm, like Doedale-griff near Levisham for example.   It is a farm village of a dozen houses, lying a little backward from the shore at the foot of a picturesque glen, along one side of which the railway from Saltburn winds to save an "incline."

Ironstone is got close by and shipped in the bay. At the date of Camden's Britannia it was a small village, flourishing by the great variety of fish it took.

Beyond Skiningrave lies Rockcliff, and the path skirts the tops of precipices, against the bases of which the sea breaks 600 feet below. In many parts we found no more space between the boundary wall of the fields and the edge of the upright cliff, than was needed for the feet, and some of us were led for assurance of safety to hold by the wall. These cliffs, partly from their perishable nature and partly from alum workings, are continually falling; but for folk with steady heads this is one of the finest walks in the county. The alum house is half way down the long steep bank which ends at the Staithes hollow, a good two miles from the high point of Boulby.

The romantic, old fashioned, Staithes cannot be seen until we are in it, for this little town, which is flavorous at the proper season with the appropriate smell of fish, and shelters about 1400 people, is built below the level of the cliffs, against the almost perpendicular banks of a short creek, shaped like a horse shoe with the circular end to the ocean, not, I think, above 350 yards across in any part; and into it and out of it we must go by roads that are nearly as steep as the roofs of the houses, unless, indeed, we enter or leave by the sea, which few do except from necessity or in the way of their occupation. The cliffs are of the ironstone series; and bending round on the north-west like a hook, protecting the houses on that hand, is Colborn nab, a screed of cliff perhaps 100 feet high and as many broad, which the sea on one side beats against and wastes, and which has on the other the little beck that "gives life and picturesque beauty to Staithes." South-east is the hard rocky cove, one eighth of a mile across from cliff to cliff, out of which Staithes looks to the sea over the rough scars and broken waves of its dangerous shore. The ordinary tides come almost up to the houses and the sea is continually making breaches. On ground, now covered by shingle, houses and shops and a sea wall stood fifty years back. There was the drapery and grocery shop kept by Saunderson, whom Captain Cook served for eighteen months in his youth, but, about 1812, the sea broke in and Mr. Saunderson's successor removed stock and furniture, took the stones of the building, and rebuilt the shop in Church street, where it may still be seen. One of the forward houses was an inn, and the inn-keeper of sixty years ago used to drive wooden wedges into the wall when he saw a stone loose; and the present keeper of the "Cod and Lobster," at this day the most advanced house in Staithes, lives in equal anxiety, for more than once the circular wall before his inn has been washed down, the last time about 1862, when, in a high storm, buildings much farther back were in the water ; and the existence of the street behind depends on his wall.

The fishermen of Staithes are strong, brave men, intelligent, and of decided character ; and the women are as helpful and as handy as they, taking active part in carrying out the nets and spreading them on the beach or cliff to dry and in other necessary operations on land. Sixteen yawls belong to Staithes, each carrying ten men and boys, and in the same months when these are employed twenty cobles, manned by three men each, are used. These figures give a total of 220 fisher. men. Add about 80 for persons otherwise connected with fishing and 100 for fish buyers and curers, and say 600 for the families, and we account for two-thirds of the population. The rest are ship owners, tradesmen, workmen, and their families. The sixteen large boats ought to earn at least £20 a week each or £320, and the twenty cobles at least £6 a week each or £120, making, per week, £2 a man or £440 ; but sometimes they earn twice. or thrice as much. The week of our visit, at the end of August, 1864, was a bad one, for the wind blew strongly from the north-east, so that only the large boats could safely go out, and they were not always successful, whereby the week's earnings were £100 less than they ought to have been. One of us went down in the morning to see what herrings were in, but the boats then arriving had none; and, as a fish buyer said, " Neen at t'other ed neen; bud ah eerd somebody saying as ah coom doon t' street, Mark ed six or seven thoosand—oo monny es eh ?" to which another answered,—" Aboot five unerd ah eerd !" The herring season is the best time of the fishermen's year. From about February to November, the large boats go out, and in the other months the same crews fish with smaller boats. We counted nearly seventy cobles lying on shore, keels upward, many of which belong to these men. Staithes is well-known throughout the eastern coast of England and Scotland, and in many inland parts. Several West-riding towns receive fish from it, and I am told that Staithes haddocks are notable for good size and quality. Much fish is salted and dried in the air, heads included, before sale, and long white rows of it are seen stretched on rods upon the cliffs. Staithes having no safe anchorage the yawls when unemployed, as from Saturday morning to Sunday evening, are taken into the little Rosedale wyke, a mile and a half southeast, where they can lie under protection of piers built for shipping ironstone of Lord Normanby's, got out of mines under the cliff. Fifteen of the yawls sailed round on the Saturday as we walked over from Staithes.

A fisherman must have pleasures, but he lives a life of hard work and danger, out night long at all seasons in his narrow boat. Those who strive in this way, manfully providing for wives and children, and often risking their lives, may be rough, but they cannot be bad men. Professor Phillips, writing of the "familiar hazard" run by the bold fishers of Flamborough, which is equally true of the Staithes men whom he happily styles "athletic Norwegian forms," notices how they set forth in their little cobles to visit perhaps the Dogger bank, possibly to return no more, *the sea gat him* being too often the reply to inquiry for some honest fisherman who may have been your boatman or your guide ! See *Rivers &c., of Yorkshire, p.* 129. The Staithes people have been described as foolishly superstitious; but one, born in the little gorge and now out in the great world, who has communicated with me, denies this. He declares that they abstain from work on Sundays and like days, not from fear, but out of a proper feeling of the sacredness of these days; whilst the assertions of their having childish fears of ghosts, and of their anticipating evil if the first morning face they meet be a woman's, he says are absurd. I cannot use his straightforward expressions, but may let him say in the spirit, and some of the words, of the *Middlesbrough News*, which he extracts, that the bold fishers of Staithes are generous to a fault and honest even to self-sacrifice; that they are kindly affectioned one to another to an extent not easy for people differently reared to appreciate; and that they pursue their enterprise with such a co-operative spirit as to have interests in the truest way common, and are partners in so many sea adventures that family is knit to family by a community of woes and blessings.

The cliffs ascend considerably from Staithes toward Rosedale wyke, forming bold prominences. The Old Nab, half a mile from Staithes, is breaking off, large blocks being detached and ready to come down. Hinderwell, a mile from Rosedale, is the Staithes burial place; and in the churchyard is St. Hilda's well, which supplies the villagers with water. A long mile eastward lies Runswick, a fine bay open to the north, about a mile across, with an inward sweep of two miles. The sloping banks, furrowed by rains, are large enough to hold a town of 5000 people; but the village is stuck on ledges in a nook, whilst the houses are connected by footways and steps that go up and down from door to door. A steep carriageway leads down to the sands. There is no horse and cart in the place, and only ten fishing cobles, and a population of about 410. The houses are below the cliffs, and, coming from the west, we are directly over the roofs. Slips sometimes occur, and one occasion is recorded when all the village went down. In the shale, across the bay, are the caves called *hob-holes*; and at the corner of a deep furrow, the footpath goes up the steep and slippery Claymoor bank, and thence through fields to Goldsborough and Lyth. Climbing *Claymer* bank was found a serious business by some of us. A farmer said the road did not please anybody, but we all got up, and I hope those who liked it least may live long to remember it. We had pleasant views on our way of the broad blue sea with numerous ships, for the wind had changed and was now off the land ; and we passed several tumuli, on one of which, remarkable for its size and position, stood a quiet horse, patiently enjoying the splendid outlook over land and sea.

We went into Mulgrave park by the Lyth gate and walked through the grounds to the ruins of the old castle, a mile or so from the present house ; saw the fine prospects down the slopes to the sea, and to Whitby, with its abbey and lighthouses, and looked into the deep and woody glens that cross the park. The castle ruins rest in woods, and there is a good view from them up the valley to the moor, but the walls and spaces are almost hidden by trees and covered with litter and weeds. Lyth stands on a hill, which ends in the alum shale rocks of Sandsend ness, where are alum works. The alum house is at Sandsend, the last sea side village of Cleveland, a tidy place contrasted with Staithes and Runswick, most of the residents of which are employed in alum making. A little further on is East Row beck, the Cleveland boundary, and stepping across that, we entered the liberty of

Whitby strand at Dunsley bay, and from there walked along the cliffs into Whitby.

The strata of the Cleveland coast are described in Professor Phillips's books; and very fully in Mr. J. G. Baker's *North Yorkshire*, a series of studies of botany, geology, climate, and physical geography, with illustrative maps, published in 1863, and from these we may learn minutely, what I transfer broadly, that the low cliffs between the Tees and Saltburn are drifted clay and pebbles resting on lias, with hard, firm, continuous sands spreading from their foot. The inferior portion of Huntcliff is lower lias shale, and the upper hard ironstone and marlstone, surmounted by a cap of glacial diluvium. The cap of Boulby cliff is of the hard arenaceous beds of the lower oolite; and the lower part shews an excellent section of the lias from its latest deposits to a depth of 100 feet in the lower shale. At Staithes, where the cliffs descend, the sandstone cap is removed and, as already noticed, the strata are of the ironstone series. Between here and Runswick the cliffs have the general character of a lias base with a sandstone covering, whilst in this bay a part of the lias shale, which lies over the ironstones that are at the base of the cliffs, stands prominent. From Kettleness to Sandsènd gritstone covers the lias.

Redcar, Saltburn, Staithes, Lyth and Whitby have good inns. This is a two days walk.

VII.

WHITBY; AND THE SEA COAST FROM WHITBY TO SCARBOROUGH AND FILEY.

Whitby; town and people — Church, abbey, hall, piers, vessels — The Scoresbys and Whaling — Modern fishery—Pilots — Jet — "Snake" stones and "thunder bolts" — Scars — Things of the shore — Whitby Strand — Cliffs — High Whitby lights — Hawsker bottoms—Robin Hood's bay; twisting streets —The Peak—Staintondale—Cloughton Moor a "caud, wild, wilderness country"—Ancient circle at Hulleys —Raven hill—Base cliff—Hayburn Wyke—Luscious gorse—Cloughton bay — Scalby ness—Scarborough; castle, town, and churches—Oliver's Mount - Cayton bay—Redcliff—Filey—Pickering vale runs out to cliffs.

WHITBY is said to be the wealthiest town of its size in Yorkshire. Certainly it would not be easy to find, elsewhere, more seemingly prosperous tradesmen. Nearly all the respectable shopkeepers are tenants of their own trade buildings, and not a few live in little mansions away from their places of business. Many of these, as well as others who have retired from

G 2

the more active conduct of affairs, are ship
owners; and numerous ships belong to the port,
which is also of considerable note as a fishing
town.   Whitby is remarkable too for the Jet
trade, a branch of industry carried on to a slight
extent at a few other places on the coast, but
which is here the peculiar, if not the staple,
trade; meets us on every hand, and affects the·
life of a great part of the population.   On
occasional visits in past years I always found the
jet trade, the herring fishery, and the stir of
shipping prominent features, together giving life
to the town and creating continual activity
throughout the narrow, irregular streets and
passages, and among the ascending tiers of
houses in the old town.   And these are still of
much interest; but great changes are going on :
the town seems no longer a remote place; the
people are fast losing the quaint and homely
character which appeared to distinguish them
from the inhabitants of much-frequented towns.
The alteration seems clear to me; and I am told
by residents that the Whitby of 1866 really does
differ materially from the Whitby of 1860.
Extensive iron furnaces are at work and prepar-
ing at Grosmont, Glaisdale end and Beckhole,
with new populations, for whom Whitby is the
market.   We hear much, too, of what the
Railway company have done and projected, and
the powerful effects their operations must have
on the trade, extent and character of the town—

the deviation to escape the incline; the new North Yorkshire and Cleveland railway; the docks and ways on the western side, with other improvements and extensions. There is expectation also of coast lines of railway. And with all this we find a great increase of sea side visitors. We shall soon be compelled to go to Robin Hood's bay and Staithes to learn what Whitby was; but even these nooks will probably not be left long as they are. Amidst all changes, however, we shall still have the measured washing of the sea on the beach in calm weather, and its roar in storms, when the waves dash against the huge cliffs, and strike with tremendous thuds into the hollows in rocks and sea wall that stand in their way.

The town is built along the mouth of the Esk, a comparatively small stream not navigable when the tide is out, flowing almost due north into the sea; and the two sides are joined by a draw bridge, the passage between the buttresses of which connects the outer and inner harbors. The east side is nearly a mile long; and, with recent buildings, the west cannot be less. The latter has most dwellings and largest population, the best streets being built upon the west cliff. On the east cliff which is the higher of the two (about 180 feet, the west being about 140) stands the old church, said to date from about 1100, fitted up like a ship and built low as if to prevent the wind blowing it off, and to get at which

nearly 200 steps must be climbed from the stair
foot, the latter itself elevated many yards above
the piers.   A hundred yards behind the church
are the ruins of the abbey of St. Hilda (a notable
personage in this neighborhood) not so old, it is
thought, as the church; built of a brown freestone, now much broken up; very picturesque
as seen from various parts of the surrounding
country and a good land mark to mariners ; but
which when seen closely looks bare.   Whitby
hall, adjoining the abbey and probably built
with abbey stone, is not an attractive mansion.
It is owned by the Cholmley family ; and was for
a long time untenanted.   It is said they intend
to repair it and live there.   Between the abbey
and church, on the abbey plain, stands an
ancient cross which Dr. Young believed to have
been the cross of the burial ground, outside
which it stands.

The Whitby piers are of vast interest to the
people and have been so for centuries.   It was
by building sea walls that the sand was got out
of the narrow spaces along the shores of the
Esk ; and from small beginnings the present
remarkable structures have grown.   The western
pier runs almost straight out to the sea for nearly
half a mile from the bridge, and forms the main
promenade of the inhabitants.   Every body
comes there and it is busy all day.   On fine
evenings a continued stream of people, young
and old, goes to the pier end where the largest

lighthouse is erected, and back again. The chief of the east piers sets out at a right angle from the end of the east cliff, and approaches the west pier so as to leave between them a narrow entrance from the sea. A lighthouse stands on this also. The other eastern piers are the burgess and fish piers, set halfway into the outer tidal passage. The east side is not easily got at, and few people go along the Haggerlyth and down the wooden cliff ladder connecting the pier with the cliff, though in blowy weather at high water it is very fine to stand there and see the waves beat into the cliff.

The total number of vessels registered at this port at the end of March 1865 was, I am told, 410; tonnage 72,809 which, calculated at six pounds a ton, makes £436,854.

Years ago—when William Scoresby the elder became a Whitby sailor, and thenceforward through the time of his thirty successful voyages ending in 1823, and through the time of the voyages of his equally successful son, Captain William the younger, afterward the Rev. William Scoresby D.D. vicar of Bradford, both fine fellows and, in a sense, Whitby men—Whitby vessels were employed in the Greenland whale fishery; but this trade ceased from here about 1838. Now the fishermen catch cod, ling, and herrings. I am told this branch of industry has largely increased in late years; that at least 100 boats small and large carrying from three to

eight men and boys a piece belong to the town;
and that fifty small boats manned not by regular
fishermen, but by pilots, ship carpenters, and
others of different occupations, go out "trunking," that is, setting and taking up hazle traps
called *pots* for catching crabs and lobsters;
whilst twenty more, manned in the same way,
are employed in catching salmon on the rocks of
the scar.   Beside these, hundreds of "craft" from
Yorkshire fishing towns and villages, and places
farther north, and large boats from the south
east coast and from Cornwall, come here in the
herring season.   It is entertaining to stand on
the pier as the boats arrive and see the fish sales
made by the auctioneers.   Full of interest, too,
are the ways of the authorized pilots, a body of
excellent men ; and of the crews of vessels from
other ports, home and foreign, to be seen here.

The jet trade employs many miners; and, it may
be, a thousand men and boys at the manufacture.
Their earnings are said to range from sixty
shillings a week to three or four, and the value
of the produce to amount to more than £20,000
a year.   This mineral, consisting of a soft and a
hard kind, the last the most valuable, is got out
of the upper lias bed along the coast and is
usually worked by drifting.   There is no certainty
of finding it in remuneration quantity, and this
gives to the getting a speculative character.   I
have heard of great successes, and have had the
fortunate men pointed out ; also of disastrous

failures—men toiling for weeks for a few shillings, and going on in the hope of making up for ill spent time and capital, but only to lose finally all they had. The largest profits are said to be made by those who buy from the miners. Great improvement has taken place in the manufacture in late years. Beautiful designs, natural or artistic, are now wrought out ; and the day of "quaker bonnets" and "buoys," once, with beads, almost the only forms in use, has gone by ; whilst fossils such as ammonites and nautilites, found in the lias, are made up with jet into many kinds of ornaments. The tools too are better than formerly, but these are only needed of a simple character—chisels and knives to block out and carve with, and lathes for grinding into shape and polishing. A few persons earn money by searching for fossils in the cliffs and scar, which are particularly rich in "snake stones" and "thunder bolts," as well as rarer things. Numerous specimens of "huge ammonites and the first bones of Time" may be seen in the museum on the pier ; and if anybody likes to buy fossils, which I believe no thorough-bred geologist does, he may do so from regular dealers.

Below the eastern cliffs are no sands ; but there, flat lias scars form a grand, though rough, walk at low water. The sands are on the west under the low diluvial cliffs which lie between Whitby and Sandsend ; and here the sea bathing

takes place. The shales and sandstone, corres-
pondent with the strata of the eastward cliffs
and Sandsend ness, are thrown down for about
three miles between these two points; and
the Esk flows over the eastern line of the
dislocation.

There is perhaps no place on the coast which
within the space of a few miles possesses more
interesting things than this. I say *more*
advisedly, because all this part of the county—
Redcar, Saltburn, Staithes, Whitby, Scarborough,
Filey—is full of attractions, and much of what is
here written about the objects of the shore will
apply to all these places. The valley of the Esk is
very beautiful, and so are the dales through
which flow its tributary becks. Walks, drives,
and railway excursions may be taken west, north
or south, so as to fill up a holiday time most
pleasantly—as, for instance, by the beck whereon
lie the Larpool woods, and Cock mill with the
foss in a pretty dell, and Rigg mill in a glen
among trees—along Little beck from Falling
foss in the Newton house grounds and thence
through Iburndale to Sleights—to Woodlands
and Aislaby—to Egton and Egton bridge and
Glaisdale end—up the Murk Esk to Beck hole
and Grosmont—to Mulgrave and Lyth—and a
score other places.

To dwellers in inland towns nothing appears
more wonderful than the (to us) strange things
upon the sea shore; and the great places for

these are the broad, flat, lias scars, and the sea-washed cliffs about Saltwick and below Hawsker bottoms, with their intervening bays where the tides come, creating danger for unskilled or careless ramblers, but giving life to countless animals and plants which, without these beneficent visitings, must perish. How delightful to come to the haunts of those comical beings the crabs—hermit, edible or dogger—and see how eagerly the frightened things hide themselves, or cranch under sheltering stones, or, with threatening claws, "stand upon their deliverance" if caught unawares or turned out of their holes. How interesting to find the long-named "anemonies," and watch them slowly distend their soft-looking, but unrelenting, tentacles; to see the apparently motionless, five-fingered star fish or the sun star, lying flat on the stones or the sand, or their irritable relative the brittle-star, which will jerk itself to bits on slight provocation; to note the common limpets, locally *flithers*, and the winkles, or *cuvvins*, which poor people and children collect and boil to sell at street corners; the trochi, the welks, and the countless acorn-barnacles adhering to the stones. What delight, also, town-bred visitors have in the sea urchins; the jelly fish, called on this coast *blubber-hunters*, pretty in the water, but helpless masses when cast out, commonly seen under these cliffs as waifs of the deep —in the shells of the rare cowrie and the cockle; the shrimps and sand-skippers and a score other things. What prizes, too, are the sea plants—the huge tangle and the streaming sea-belt, known here as *reck*, sure weather-gauges when hung in the passages at home; the bladder fucus which cracks beneath the feet; the green and brown lavers; the deep-water rhodosperms, to which belong the beautiful delesserias and the brittle corallines, plants which in a general way are only seen afloat, drifting into hollows, and which change their place with change of wind, for most of them are not native here but come from afar with the tides. Many of the plants, also, which grow on and near the shore are curious—as the sea buckthorn; the grass of parnassus; the sand-staying bents; the thick leaved scurvy grass, sea sand-wort, and milkwort; the sea rocket, wild celery, and michaelmas daisy. But whether the tourist stay by the ever attractive sea, or strike into the vales or over the moorlands, he may spend happy and profitable days hereabout, if not too indifferent or too proud to find pleasure in the ways of humble people, shrewd as himself though different in manners, or in things of a lower order of life, or in geologizing, botanizing, brambling, mushrooming, or other out-of-door pursuit.

The broad liberty of Whitby Strand, which once belonged to St. Hilda's Abbey and is seventeen miles long and from three to seven

wide, stretches from East Row beck at Sandsend,
to within four miles of Scarborough, taking in the
coast as far, almost, as the Peak at Robin Hood's
bay; strikes across country southward, to within
about a mile to the west of Scalby; includes
Hackness; then goes up the Derwent and over
the moors to Grosmont, and follows from there
the Cleveland boundary to the sea again.

Starting from Whitby to go southward we
pass the old church and the ruined abbey, and
see in many places signs of late falls of the
cliffs. Once, they say, the abbey stood a good
distance from the sea. Now its ruins are not
above the fourth of a mile from high water; and
year after year the tides and the air bring down
the cliffs and extend the broad floor of lias
scars at the foot. We soon pass the black and
wasting alum shale nab at Saltwick and the bay
itself; and, two and a half miles from Whitby,
come to the Beacon hill, below which stand the
two High-Whitby lighthouses finished and first
lighted in October 1858. These, with their
dwellings and inclosures, appear dangerously
close to the almost perpendicular and crumb-
ling cliff. As we stand upon projections from
the narrow strip of land in front of the inclosures
and watch the flying gulls, that look like silvered
crosses, set out from the rocks beneath us, and
see the white edge of the rising tide 300 feet
down, we think it would be safer to live in a
house farther back; but the builders no doubt

knew their business and satisfied themselves that the sandstone foundation was not likely to be washed away for many years. A mile and a half farther, lie the pastures called Hawsker bottoms, where the ground is depressed toward the sea. Hawsker village, a poor looking place, stands a mile inland and a rather deep and wooded beck, called Raw pasture beck, flows through one of the hollows and falls over on to the sea shore. Then the cliffs rise again to the bold prominence called Bay ness, but soon descend abruptly and come almost down to the beach at Bay town.

The latter was anciently, as I read, called Fyling; but has been known as Robin Hood's bay from at least as far back as the *Itinerary* of Leland, "begunne about 1538," when it was "a Fischer Tounlet of 20 Bootes," and there was "a Dok or Bosom of a mile yn lenghth;" and when at "Whiteby" was "an havenet holp with a peere and a great fischar Toune." The Bay town and Flying-thorpe, half a mile inland, lie in a depression along which a little beck flows. As we go down the cliffs the broad bay lies before us, a three miles sweep from nab to nab, with its narrow belt of sand and hard floor of lias rocks fronting the sea in successive and slightly inclined curves; and at its southern limit stand the giant cliffs of the peak more than 500 feet high. There are some good houses on the top of the bank as we go down into the bay,

for this little town is rich and has great interests
in shipping; and there is an appearance of
prosperity in the two narrow and steep streets of
fifteen feet width, and the more numerous
pebble-paved, twisting, byeways and passages,
of from three to six feet wide, which compose
this old fashioned place. It is very like Staithes,
only better built; and not unlike what Whitby
was, but smaller. We enter by a road down a
steep bank and find the houses erected on the
little nabs, upon the two sides of the beck which
flows through the midst. The houses are piled
up the banks rank over rank, separated only by
the narrow passages just mentioned; and we see
all sorts of boxing-off and contrivances to save
room, as if the people lived in a ship and must
have plenty of "lockers." Here is very little
fishing now; no yawl; only six or seven cobles,
and not twenty regular fishermen, whilst a dozen
or so employ themselves in "trunking." Most
of the young men go to sea in sailing ships.
Many of the ships owned here are in the coasting
and Baltic trades.

The cliffs on the round of the bay are only
about 100 feet high, the base being lower lias
rock and the upper parts a soft diluvial stratum,
constantly perishing. The way up to Raven hill
passes near the line of a dislocation of strata and
up a steep cliff of the alum shale, and brings us
to the high grounds where the once extensive
Peak alum works were, and to the elevated Stoup

brow with its tumuli; and to the rugged mounds
and glens of the hill, in parts of which oak and
other trees grow and where we find broad
patches of yellow broom and gorse. Here too
are jet drifts; and the mansion called Raven
hall (a house of Mr. Hammond's) to the owner-
ship of which is now added a "great weight of
moor." At Greendike, ends the coast boundary
of Whitby Strand; and we enter the liberty of
Pickering Lyth shortly after leaving the level of
the bay, and continue therein until we arrive at
the point of the romantic Filey Brig.

Parallel with the sea coast, and commencing
half a mile or thereabout from Raven hill, lies
the uneven surface of Staintondale. The village
of the same name, where the school house is, the
best thing in it, lies two miles farther down; and
the deep and wooded glen through which
Hayburn beck flows, lies four miles from the
Peak. On one occasion, I walked through the
dale and, striking off the road beyond Hayburn
beck, went up Cloughton moor and by the farm
called Hulleys—here *hullos*—to Cloughton village. It was a cloudy day and the moor looked
dreary. An old resident, with whom I met, said,
"It's a caud, wild, wilderness country up o'
Cloughton moor. T' wind lists up 'ere, an
wheear t' wind lists, it blaws. Yeh knaw Moses
ses seeah. Don't yeh knaw Cloughton?"—No
this is my first visit.—"Deeary me, deeary me;
ah mun gang an shew yeh t' road."—No, no! I

can find my way.—" It 'll do meh good to gang
doon wi yeh. Yeh knaw scripter says, if ony
body axes yeh to gang a mile wi' 'im gang wi'
'im tweea."—Aye, aye.—" Yeh knaw Moses says
seeah. It 'll do meh good. Ah's seventy eight,
an ah's seean 'a done 'ere mebbe ; ah's seean 'ev
a new life." So I could not refuse the old man's
help, but let him guide me down the slack and
talk his kindly and hopeful talk, intermixed
with fragments of scripture and odd lines from
Wesley's hymns, till we came to the second or
third wall, where he blessed me and turned back
singing a hymn as he went, as blithely as a lad.
In the hollow of the moor, a quarter of a mile
below the Hulleys, and close to the little grip
which lower down becomes a beck, is the
"druidical" circle of stones, seven yards in
diameter with a hollow near the centre of it,
referred to in a preceding walk ; and on the
higher ground to the west are said to be
intrenchments, tumuli and pits, indicating the
site of a British village, things, as frequently
stated, very common on these moors. The
large and apparently prosperous villages of
Cloughton and Burniston, lie between here and
Scarborough, about a mile from the sea cliffs.

It is, however, more interesting to walk on these
cliffs ; and, passing into the Raven hall fields, we
stand in a commanding position overlooking the
sea. Half a mile south-east is Bleawick point, the
low extremity of which the sea covers at high

water; and for two miles between this and
Petard point we have below us an undercliff,
called the Base cliff.   At that part of the latter
which lies beyond the little tarns marked on the
ordnance map, the upright face of the cliff and
the level of the undercliff are richly covered with
gorse, underwood and trees.   The trees reach to
the very top, and are there flattened and stretched
backward over the land by force of the sea
breezes, in a curious manner.   In some instances
the hawthorns are fifteen or sixteen feet long.
These cliffs and the steep banks of Hayburn
wyke, locally miscalled *Abram* wyke, were very
beautiful in the leafy month of June.   Hayburn
beck flows in a deep channel from a considerable
distance inland, and the glen is filled with trees,
which extend over the face of the south eastern
bank to the point called Little cliff, covering the
ground, except in a few places where the surface
was yellow with gorse flowers or bright with rich
grass.   Wild plants grow luxuriantly at the
bottom of the valley and in the woods.   The
strawberry, wood violet, and several of the
orchids are very fine and so are many of the
commoner ferns; whilst here, and everywhere
in our present walk on and near the cliffs, the
luscious gorse filled the air with a delicious
odour and made the land glorious with its
hillocks of flowers.   There are many paths
through the woods, leading to and past Hayburn
wyke farm and on to the top of Little cliff, and

thence we see on one hand the wood and the course of the stream to the edge of the heather; and on the other the sea studded with sailing ships and steamers. In another mile we come to the irregular, stony, Cloughton bay down to which only foot passengers can go. The cliffs fall rapidly toward it, but rise again, and in the centre of the bay present a jagged front to the sea 100 feet high. Great masses of rock are constantly falling here, and it is unsafe as well as laborious to cross the rough stones which lie at the foot of this cliff. Thenceforward— through the Cloughton and Burniston fields, over Hundale point, Long nab, and Cromer point, Scalby ness and the mound at Peasholm fort, to Scarborough castle—the cliffs have an elevation of 100 feet, or less, above the sea; and for the last three miles we walk upon a clayey stratum, which the sea has broken into, especially about Scalby, where the beck flows out of a deep but uninteresting gorge and where is a great breadth of sand. The outline of the angular Peasholm fort, which Hinderwell says was one of the encampments of the Parliamentary forces when besieging the castle in 1644-5, is still distinct upon the hill about a mile from the castle.

The broad north sands of Scarborough stretch from Scalby ness to the foot of the Castle cliff, which is a bold headland near 300 feet high, crowned by the ruins of the castle Keep and of

H 2

the outer walls. From many parts of the sea
cliffs, beginning with Raven hill, the castle is a
good land mark and we see on one side of it the
great how called Oliver's Mount, anciently
Weaponness, a mile and a half southward; and
on the other the long line of coast ending at
Filey brig; and beyond that again, the still
longer promontory of Flamborough head, seventeen miles direct from the castle and twenty-five
from the high cliffs north of Hayburn wyke.
Parallel to the coast lies the high ridge of
Suffield moor, continued toward Seamer, with its
farm houses and prominent beacon, and between
that and Oliver's mount is the lake-like hollow
through which the railway goes.

There are few West-Yorkshire people who do
not know the far-famed Scarborough, the busy,
large, and constantly extending town, wherein
all classes of our population find suitable
dwellings in which to spend their leisure times.
Professor Phillips says no situation on the Yorkshire coast offers the same combination of
picturesque cliffs, convenient access, comfortable
dwellings, amusements for invalids, and motives
for exercise to the more robust, along pleasant
sands, among ancient fortifications, over prominent hills, or through woody valleys. It is
readily admitted to be supreme among northern
watering places. [*Rivers &c., of Yorkshire, p.*
133.] Improvements are always making; and
in the early part of the season we walk past

houses at which workmen are employed to make
them look their best. The north cliff terraces
have been erected in late years and so have the
mansions on the south cliff, where dwell the
really fashionable folk; while on the south-
western side of the town, under the shadow of
Oliver's mount, a new district has still more
recently grown up and has been made easily
accessible from the railway station by means of
the new bridge. In striking contrast with all
this, is the dismantled castle, with its moskering
coat of arms on the entrance tower, type of the
rest of this old structure; its cloven keep, and
the lowered walls, broken and decayed. Below
the castle cliff lie the piers, which afford little
shelter in storms and are nearly always busy.
We found numerous signs of a wealthy population—the many lodging houses, inns, shops and
public buildings; the bright, newly painted
houses, shining in the morning sun; the well
kept Cliff bridge with the contiguous esplanade,
saloons, music hall, prospect tower, and paths
winding along the grassy face of the cliff among
trees and beds of ferns and flowering plants;
the new bridge before named; the magnificent
Cliff hotel, got up by a public company, rising
from the south sands and looking down the
coast to Filey brig and Flamborough head. One
other creditable thing we noticed, too—the neat
drinking fountain on the castle cliff "To the
memory of T. Hinderwell the historian of

Scarborough and founder of its museum" erected in 1860 by "some who knew and loved him." Scarborough may become remarkable for its churches and chapels, though one (the Rev G. A. Poole) who regards the church as the only thing which consecrates the scene and gives it its crowning beauty, says the Scarborough of to-day is sadly inferior to the Scarborough of former ages. The choir of the parish church is in ruins, having been battered down by Sir Hugh Cholmley and his garrison 200 years ago, when attempting to drive off their enemies who are described as firing cannon out of the east window; and the main tower, therefore, which once stood in the centre now stands at the east end. There have been western towers. The building is irregular and the several portions differ from each other in style. The most singular parts are the chapels on the south side with their heavy stone roofs. In the new town at the foot of Oliver's Mount we saw an elaborate gothic building in course of erection to be used as a chapel by the Independent Dissenters. It quite eclipses the plainly built church of St. Martin's close by.

Leaving Scarborough we climbed to the top of the steep Mount and viewed thence the ground walked over the previous day from the Peak to Scarborough castle, with broad surface of the north eastern moors far away inland, whilst in the other direction lay the sea coast down to Filey. Three miles to the south east lies Cayton bay where the Scarborough water-works are situate, a fine spring here throwing out a quantity of water more than sufficient for the great town. Cayton bay has a sandy shore and good sites for dwellinghouses. Still following the coast we come to the bold Redcliff and the Wyke, from which sets out the ness called Club point, the sides of which are rapidly falling. It is a pleasant walk from Redcliff to the long projection of hard rocks constituting Filey brig, where the upper stratum of clayey diluvium which presents a curiously streaked appearance when seen from Filey sands, is constantly wasting under the influence of rain and wind. Some time, perhaps before long, these agencies and the sea will cut the ness in two; probably remove it altogether and add its rocky base to the bridge. At low water the narrow line of rocks which constitutes the "brig" stretches half a mile into the sea and forms the great attraction of the place; and very interesting it is on fine days to walk about there, and watch the ships sailing by out at sea, and the fishermen's boats moving off the point or steering about the great bay; and to see the clear water lave the hard sides of the rocks, making one in hot weather long to be cooled in it. Ten miles south east of the brig, across the bay, lies the long promontory of Flamborough Head, the cliffs of which stand against the bay like a l····

wall. Fishing is the chief trade of Filey, and we were told it has about twenty seven yawls and twenty four cobles and perhaps 300 fishermen. We could not learn that it owns ships. Filey is in two separate portions, called the old and new towns, and these are not properly connected by roads. The broad Vale of Pickering runs out to the cliffs at Filey and the coast line of the north eastern moorlands ends here. At a distance of four or five miles from Filey brig we leave the strata of which the moors are composed; for the southern side of the bay consists of chalk and belongs to the wolds.

Whitby, Robin Hood's bay, Scarborough and Filey are good places to stay at. Three or four days, or more, ought to be allowed for the towns and cliffs here described.

VIII.

FILEY TO HACKNESS AND CROSS CLIFF — SALT-
ERSGATE TO LILHOE CROSS AND SLEIGHTS—
CAWTHORN CAMPS—PICKERING.

Filey to Seamer—Ayton castle—Forge valley—Hackness
—Silpho moor—Langdale — Moorland edges — Cross
cliff—Blakey Topping—Bridestones—Hole of Horcum
—Whinny Neb—Lilhoe cross — Source of Derwent—
Falling foss—Iburndale—Esk and Newton dales —
Cawthorn camps—Pickering, castle, church.

SEAMER JUNCTION, on the northern side of the Vale of Pickering,
lies six miles from Filey, and the
railway passes through a flattish,
farming, country between the two great ranges
of hills, the moors and the wolds. Having
reached the junction, we walked to the ruined
keep of Ayton castle, which stands in beautiful
sloping pastures on the right bank of the
Derwent, at the foot of Forge valley; and thence

up the valley itself to Hackness. This beautiful
vale of the Derwent is narrow for nearly two
miles, and the steep sides are covered with
forest trees. A short distance past the forge
houses, it widens and is very pleasant, the lower
portions of the slopes being rich grass fields, and
the upper planted with trees.

The country about Hackness, the name of
which, they say, means the *cloven points*, both that
part the Scarborough visitors pass through and
that which they do not usually see is very
beautiful. The northern portion is a distinct
patch of moor from two to three miles broad and
five long, standing boldly over the surrounding
land at elevations above the sea, varying from
100 or 200 to 700 feet. Down the western side
of this, the river Derwent, after leaving its source
on the desolate moors between High Woof howe
and Lilhoe cross, flows briskly away. Many
steep dales meet at Hackness, like the outspread
fingers of a hand leading down into the palm.
The longest of those that occupy the centre
extend about two and a half miles. Many are
much shorter. The principal have bright little
becks in them; the others are dry and steep
glens; nearly all are planted with trees in the
upper portions, and grow rich grass in the lower.
Hackness hall stands in a delightful park in the
midst, surrounded by an abundance of trees.
Walks through the woods on the north are left
open to the public; and it is pleasing to see the

parties of friends joyously climbing to the higher points, or resting in prominent places among the trees.

Passing on the unfrequented roads up Lowdales and Whisperdales, each having its single dwelling, where the Howe ends close down upon the valleys, we climbed the bank to Reasty top and stood on Silpho moor. The beacon on Seamer moor, which is seen from all places about Scarborough, is a distinct object from here also. We have fine views into Whisperdales on one side, and the broad and almost treeless Harwood dale on the other. Out to sea lies Cloughton wyke with the ships in full sail beyond; and, northward, the moors as far as the Peak. Coming along the Barnscliff side of the moor we pass through Broxa, and, turning toward the west, overlook Langdale, through which flows the Derwent, the line whereof is traceable by trees. The long and narrow strip of moor called Langdale side, and the isolated Howden hill, with the village of Langdale end at its foot, are just opposite to us; and beyond these, over Bickley moor, lie the conical Blakey topping, the brow of the great Cross cliff, and the projection called Whinney neb near Saltersgate. Left of these, and nearer to us, four or five howes overlook valleys down which streams flow to the Derwent. Scenes of the same character occur in other parts of these moors, where looking east and west, we see a succession of nabs fronting the north. These nabs are the ends of long moorland edges, which sweep half round wide spaces of lower ground like the shores of great bays. Cross cliff is remarkable in this respect. It makes a curve near four miles long, standing from 600 to 800 feet above the sea, and 300 to 400 above the streams at its base. The Cross cliff valley was a grand sight as we saw it, one fine sunny day, when broad patches of the steep sides were covered with the foliage of trees and bright with plants and flowers, among which the pretty *cornus suecica* was abundant. Many alders grow in the vales hereabout, and the trees are cut up into clogwood which, having been rough-shaped on the spot, is floated down the streams, caught again, and then packed off into the manufacturing towns of Lancashire and Yorkshire, where the feet of industrious people make the streets musical with it. Pity some of the pure water and fresh air cannot be sent too.

Toward the western side of the Cross cliff valley, stands the great mound called Blakey topping, a howe, as already named, like Freebrough. We went from Langdale end to Cross cliff by way of North head and the precipitous Deepdale, calling at the hospitable South moor House, where Mr. Hammersley is cultivating the high surface of the moorland ; and thence along the rough tracks to the Bridestones, as the great, natural, isolated, masses of rock, standing on the eastern banks of great and little Doedale griffs, at the head of Staindale, are called. Several of these " stones " are almost circular in form, and from ten to twenty-five yards in diameter, and perhaps ten yards high. There are two rows, ranging north and south. Some are even with the surface of the moor at the back, others stand clear above it. The rows are a hundred yards apart, and contain nine or ten weatherworn blocks a piece. One, on a narrow base, is called the " salt cellar ;" another, from which we see the Rosedale chimney, is the " church." A rough three and a half miles west, lies Levisham station, whence these curiosities are usually reached ; and two and a half north west within half a mile of the Saltersgate inn, is the great, somewhat round, Hole of Horcum, which seems the fourth of a mile or more across and 150 yards deep ; and looks, so a farmer said, as if Blakey topping had been cut out of it. Below the great hole is another large hollow and, farther down still, a green, and deep, narrow valley, through which the clear little Levisham beck flows, between the farms of Lockton and Levisham, to join the Pickering beck at the foot of Newton dale.

From the Inn at Saltersgate a track leads up the moor to Whinny neb and Cross cliff, and, following this, we come to the foot of Blakey topping. Three or four miles due north, through uneven ground, knee deep in heather and boggy, stands the dark looking Lil-hoe or Lil-howe, nearly 1000 feet above the sea, with its ancient, but lately rifled, tumulus and tall stone cross. This is the most elevated point between Newton dale, the Esk, and the sea. About it are lower heights of the same dreary aspect, also crowned with tumuli; and in the wild, treeless, moorland hollow, between it and High Woof howe, lies, as before mentioned, the source of the river Derwent. Many miles of moor are visible from here, and many known points. Continuing nearly due north for another three miles, we come to the wooded glen of May-becks, where forest trees grow very well, and which furnishes a striking contrast to the brown, heathery surfaces on the east, west, and south of it. This is the head of the valley wherein Newton house and the villages of Little-beck and Iburndale lie. A mile down we arrive at one of the principal waterfalls in the district, Falling foss, which has a descent of, probably, thirty feet; and thence pass through a deep and narrow dale, one side clothed with wood, to a cliff of alum shale, and refuse banks of old alum workings, where are mounds and glens and steep slopes of yellow broom, with heights crowned with trees, at the foot whereof lie the dwellings of Littlebeck. Forward, past Iburndale to Sleights station, the stream continues very pretty. The lower part of the valley is considerably wider than the upper, and when we were there it was delightfully scented by great quantities of flowers.

There does not appear to be any road, except the railroad, along the winding valleys which lie between Grosmont and Pickering. Travelling by railway we see them pretty well. Below Grosmont the valley of the Esk is a beautiful dale, rich with foliage, made richer still in the spring by bushes of yellow broom, and white hawthorn. Between Grosmont and the moor top, we have views of considerable extent; and though the country is rugged, it has short pretty dells with trees and slopes of grass. Next appears a space of bare moorlands and peat bogs, where the waters collect and the streams begin to flow both ways; then we run on into Newton dale, winding now past dark heathery prominences, or bare limestone cliffs, and broad patches of gorse; and, after those, between steep grassy banks or wooded slopes, with valleys opening through them. The glen down which Levisham beck comes is one of the most picturesque of these.

Two and a half miles westward of Levisham station, through Newton village, and along the top of Rawcliff, are the Cawthorn camps, four in number, through which the Roman way passed to and from Dunsley wyke. They stand upon the high edge of the cliff, which here makes a steep descent toward the north, like Cross cliff and others of the same configuration which

stretch east and west along this part of the
moors, though the land, generally, rises 400 or
500 feet from here to the Cleveland hills. The
most westerly camp stands 650 feet above the
sea, and perhaps 150 above the foot of the cliff;
and all four decline to the south, overlooking a
wide expanse of country, the Vale of Pickering
and the northern slope of the wolds being within
view on that side, whilst, north and west, the
moors to an equal extent are seen. The inside
of each camp lies so as to be observable from the
others and, excepting some parts, the surface
slopes pretty uniformly to the south. All have
distinct outlines, and are surrounded by ditches.
An intrenchment runs along the brow of the
cliff and continues beyond the camps westward;
and we see where the road went down the cliff
and up the rise to the places now called Stape
and Mauley Cross. The three eastward camps
are rudely formed, with a single trench. Each
of the first two is about 600 feet square; the
next, an oval, is perhaps 750 by 350. The
westerly camp, described as the permanent
station, is about 500 feet square, is more care-
fully laid down, and has a double ditch and
broad interspace, with level ways through the
centres of three of the sides. The surfaces of all
are covered with heather. One of the series of
howes before mentioned, projecting over valleys
westward, is well seen from the camp hill.

Pickering, the capital of many moorland, as

well as lowland, villages and farms, looks clean
like all non-manufacturing towns in limestone
districts. Its castle, occupying high ground
over the valley through which the Pickering
beck flows, is the most attractive thing in it to
people who go there for pleasure. The clumsy
door at the contracted entrance being opened by
a key ten times too big, we enter the outer court,
all round which are portions of the wall, those
on the south being good and a fair height; and
at intervals are towers shewing capital masonry.
Many staircases and passages occur in the towers;
and, it seems, a covered way, communicating with
the second floors, ran from tower to tower, along
the walls. Not much is left of the keep on the
abrupt central mound, nor of the walls formerly
connecting it with the inner towers of the fortress.
The ruins are very extensive and interesting;
and the site commands an agreeable prospect of
the woods and knolls at the lower end of Pickering vale, but we get no notion of their size or
character when passing on the railway. Pickering
church is a notable building, with its plain steeple,
amply buttressed tower, large south porch,
transepts and vestry. Inside are ancient tombs.
One, bearing the effigy of a crusader, is described
as the tomb of a Bruce. Leland in the *Itinerary*
says he saw two or three tombs belonging to the
Bruces, one whereof, lying in a chapel on the
south, bore the effigies of a man and his wife. I
believe none of the old monuments now has an

inscription, but the church keeper informs people that two recumbent figures representing a man and a woman are the effigies of John O'Gaunt and his wife.

Hackness, Saltersgate, Sleights and Pickering are the places we stayed at. The localities named were seen at twice and about four days were occupied.

IX.

THE HOWARDIAN HILLS FROM CASTLE HOWARD TO CRAYKE.

The Hills—Abbeys, castles, mansions—Kirkham Abbey
—Castle Howard—Ganthorpe—Terrington — Sheriff
Hutton—Dalby—Brandsby—River foss—Crayke; extensive prospect, castle, church—Descent to Easingwold in the vale.

GEOLOGICALLY, the tract of hilly
ground, about seventeen miles long
by six broad, lying between Malton
and Coxwold, the Vale of Pickering
and the Derwent, called the Howardian hills,
belongs to the north-eastern moors. The most
elevated portion appears from the map to be at
Yearsley, three miles south-west of Gilling, where
the height is 565 feet above the sea. The land
falls from there on all sides, more or less
gradually, and the many agreeable sites on the

I 2

undulating surfaces of the hills are occupied by parks and mansions, and by numerous villages with names ending in *ton, thorp* and *by*. The face of the land is much broken up and, walking along it, we have, alternately, extensive views disclosed and then are shut in by near elevations and woods. Very little moorland is to be found now, nearly all the ground being cultivated. I think no doubt can exist that the form which this range of heights presents has been the cause of founding upon, and at the feet of, it the great number of ancient and modern abbeys, castles and mansions here seen—Kirkham, Malton and Newburgh; Crayke, Sheriff Hutton, Gilling and Slingsby; Hovingham, Wiganthorpe, Whitwell, with others; and chief of all the stately Castle Howard, erected in place of an old castle of Hinderskelf by an earl of Carlisle 150 years ago, properly, however, not a castle but a palace; for it has none of the features of a stronghold, whereas the county does not, perhaps, possess a dwelling of greater magnificence, more richly set among ornamented grounds or more amply graced with subsidiary buildings, beautiful gardens and excellent statuary.

The few ruins of Kirkham, overgrown with ivy, and consisting of the beautiful, large gateway, part of the chancel wall, and foundations of other portions of the buildings, are seen as we pass on the railway close by the Derwent within half a mile of Castle Howard station. The reported account of its origin is the tale of an absorbing grief like that which befel the foundress of Bolton, occurring in the early part of the twelfth century, the stated names of the sufferers being Walter and Adelina Espec, to the same cause, also, being ascribed the founding, by the same Walter, of the abbey of Rievaulx. Immediately above on the east, and also directly across the river on the west, heights arise which close in the part of the valley wherein the ruins lie.

Castle Howard may be got at from this side or from Barton le street on the north. The railways pass round by Malton to the latter. Two miles from Barton, up the sloping fields that look across the vale to Helmsley, Kirkby Moorside and Pickering, and to the moors behind them, rests the grassy village of Coneysthorpe; and, a mile beyond that, the great House itself. Below the northern front of the mansion lie the lakes, occupying several hundred acres and tenanted by great numbers of wild and tame water birds, among which we counted forty swans. Beyond the water and across the park runs a long line of heights and trees and, over the lowest part of these, we see the north-eastern moors about Rosedale. The southern front of the castle, which is above one hundred yards long, is the grandest part of the building. It consists of a central pediment; two wings, along which are ranges of Corinthian pilasters; and a great central dome which rises above all with excellent effect. On, and at the sides, and in front of the large, well kept, and highly ornamented lawn rest numerous pieces of marble sculpture. These are placed, upon bases more or less elevated, in the open space as well as on the line of the inclosing walls. Beyond the inclosure extend hundreds of acres of slopes and levels of grass land with water, bridges, walks, terraces, statues and erections, among which the mausoleum, resting place of the departed Howards, the pyramid and temples are remarkable. In the distance we see the wolds. Another feature of the park is the long avenues of fine trees. Straight rows of this kind often look rigid and unnatural ; but if they ought to be approved anywhere, this is a place where people would, at least, forego objection. One way the lines extend two miles; in the other, crossing the first at a right angle, above a mile ; and at the centre stands the large obelisk erected to commemorate the great Duke of Marlborough. The magnificence of Castle Howard is not restricted to the exterior, for the fine rooms and galleries of the interior contain books, pictures, and other works of art, with rich furniture and decorations suitable to such a noble house. Some of the things here, like the painting of the three Marys, are known all over the kingdom. It is a long time since I saw over the rooms. The inn at the southern side of the park is still kept open though it seems like Castle Howard itself to have undergone a change since the death of its late noble owner, the beloved "Lord Morpeth" of the West Riding.

Ganthorpe, a mile from the inn, occupies the edge of sloping ground; and, at the distance of another mile, is the pleasant village of Terrington. From the upper end of this place Sheriff Hutton castle is seen, three miles off, and beyond it York Minster, ten miles farther. Westward lie the north-western moors, and northward the Hambletons. Nearer to us is the delightfully placed Wiganthorpe hall, which looks very pretty when seen in combination with the lake in its front and with the Castle Howard woods.

Dalby has a queer little church with a tile roof; and Brandsby, which occupies the foot of wooded hills, whence we still see York, and is situate about five miles from Terrington and two from Crayke, possesses a chapel with a dome, looking formal and cold. At a mile and a half from Brandsby, we step over the river Foss, which rises near the top of Newburgh park, not far from Yearsley, about eighteen miles from York; and very soon we come to the little town of Crayke, which occupies the hill of that name and stands about 400 feet above the sea, no great elevation, but we may ascend a hundred hills, thrice as high, without discovering such an extensive prospect as we get from this. The vast plain of York spreads out before us, bounded on one hand by the wolds, which stretch away in a long

and diminishing line from Acklam to and beyond
Pocklington and Market Weighton, until lost in
the lower ground near to the Humber; and on
the other by the north western fells, on the front
range of which we see Wensleydale, Penhill, and
the Nidd Whernsides.

In the great vale we distinguish York, Sutton-
on-the-forest, Stillington, Newton-on-Ouse,
Tollerton, Easingwold, Boroughbridge, Ripon,
Thirsk, and countless other towns and villages.
To the north lie the upper part of the vale,
drained by the Swale and the Wisk; and we see
Rolston scar, Hood hill, and the high part of
Newburgh park; nearer, Yearsley village and
the woods about Brandsby and Stearsby. The
ruins of Crayke castle stand upon the highest
part of the hill. A little away from them is
the church named after St. Cuthbert, who,
according to the Venerable Archdeacon of Cleveland the present rector of Crayke, may probably
be conjectured to have founded it, for he did
found a monastery at this place. The church,
which was enlarged two or three years ago, I
was told, and is now in excellent condition,
stands, says the rector, near the eastern extremity
of the platform on the top of the hill, a little
lower in elevation than the site of the castle; "a
neat little country church, of the age of Henry
VII., as may be judged by the style of the architecture and by the ornament of the Tudor rose
which may be seen carved in oak in a comely

chancel screen of the same age as the building itself. It is of polished stone within and without." This I take from a chapter, relating to Crayke, written for Gill's *Vallis Eboracensis*, printed in 1852. The castle itself belongs to Captain Waite, who has converted the keep into a dwellinghouse and now lives occasionally in the dark rooms. Sufficient daylight to make the apartments cheerful cannot possibly shine through the deep window openings, constructed in the thick walls. The authority just quoted remarks that the visitor will be disappointed if he look for great antiquity in the keep, now occupying the prominent portion of the hill, for the present building was evidently built after a larger fortress had been dismantled; probably in the time of the Tudor kings; but the low vaulted room, almost buried beneath the soil to the north, with its strong-ribbed arched roof, and a detached portion of ruin, inclosing a broken stair, to the north east, are remnants of a much earlier date *p.* 133.

The Hill of Crayke is at the extremity of the Howardian hills; and we speedily drop down from it into the level of the great vale, and come upon roads whence the prospect is bounded by the contiguous hedgerows, wherefore more than half the pleasure of walking, at least to those who prefer hills, will here end. The little country town of Easingwold, with its grassy streets, new, brick-built, town hall, and well placed, square-set church, stands two miles from Crayke ; and about three miles farther is Alne station, eleven miles from York, whence we travel home by railway.

Malton, Castle Howard, Crayke, and Easingwold have inns. One day and a half was the time occupied in this walk.

INDEX.

A.

Abbey plain at Rievaulx, 44.
Acklam, 118.
Adelbrough from Arncliffe, 31.
Aire river, 10.
Aislaby (near Pickering), 55; near Whitby, 88.
Alne station, 120.
Ampleforth college, 49.
Appleton-on-Wisk, 47; le moors, 54, 55, 56, 66.
Arden moor, 33, 44.
Arncliffe (Ingleby), 17, 21, 29, 31; hall, 30, 35.
———— (Eskdale) 25, 26, 63.
Ascham Roger, 19.
Ashdale, 50.
Aysdale gate, 60.
Ayton, 16, 19, 20; moor, 21, 22, 72; castle, 103.

B.

Baines's Flora of Yorkshire, 11.
Baker J. G. *(North Yorkshire)*, 80.
Bards and Authors of Cleveland, &c., 18.
Barnaby Moor, 21.
Barnscliff, 105.
Barry Sir Charles, 42.
Barton le street, 115.
Basaltic dyke, 12, 21.
Base cliff, 96.
Bay ness, 92.
Bazedale, 23; abbey, 18.
Beacon hill, High Whitby, 91.

K 2

C.

D.

E.

F.

G.

H.

I.

J.

K.

L.

M.

N.

O.

P.

Q.

R.

S.

T.

U.

V.

W.

Y.

Z.

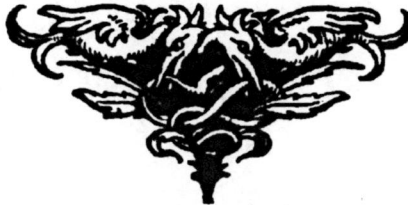

PRICE FIVE SHILLINGS,

Foolscap 8vo. neatly bound in Cloth, with two Maps prepared specially,

WALKS IN YORKSHIRE:

I.

IN THE NORTH WEST,

II.

IN THE NORTH EAST,

BY

W. S. BANKS.

ALSO

Published 1865, Foolscap 8vo, price 1s. 6d., post free from Wakefield,

PROVINCIAL WORDS

IN USE AT

WAKEFIELD,

WITH

EXPLANATIONS, INCLUDING DESCRIPTIONS OF BUILDINGS AND LOCALITIES,

COLLECTED BY

W. S. BANKS.

LONDON: J. RUSSELL SMITH, SOHO SQUARE.
WAKEFIELD: W. R. HALL, KIRKGATE.

YOUTHS RIGGED OUT FOR SEA, ANI
ALL KINDS OF CLOTHING FOI
SEA-FARING PURPOSES AT

W. DRURY'S,

OUTFITTER,

1, EASTBOROUGH,

SCARBOROUGH.

GASPERE GUARNERIO,
(From London)

4, NEWBOROUGH-ST. SCARBOROUGH,

PRACTICAL

WATCH & CLOCK MAKER,
WORKING JEWELLER, &c.

Watches and Clocks and Jewellery repaired and re-modelled by experienced workmen on the premises.

GEO. BROWN,

JET ORNAMENT MANUFACTURER,

(From Whitby)

LAND'S CLIFF,
SCARBOROUGH.

SCARBOROUGH.

——o‡o——

Good Accommodation for Visitors at the

BAR HOTEL,

TOP OF NEWBOROUGH-STREET.

TERMS—5s. 6d. per day, including attendance.

An Ordinary daily, 2s. each, at Half-past One.

An excellent Billiard Room.   Burroughs and Watts's Tables.

JOHN GIBB,

OPTICIAN TO THE ADMIRALTY,

38, *ST. NICHOLAS-STREET,*

SCARBOROUGH.

Binocular Glasses for the Field, Opera, and Seaside, in every variety.

SPECTACLES TO SUIT ALL SIGHTS.

SOLE AGENT FOR ROGERS & SONS' CELEBRATED SHEFFIELD CUTLERY.

N.B.—Sole Maker of the Celebrated Sc Telescopes, 7s. 6d. each.

To Families Visiting Scarborough.

——o‡o——

HENRY WELBURN,

(Late Z. T. Welburn)

Tea Dealer & Importer of Wines

AND SPIRITS,

ALE & PORTER MERCHANT,

55, NEWBOROUGH-STREET,

(3 doors below Queen-Street.)

GOOD DINNER CLARET DIRECT FROM BORDEAUX,
AT 10s. 6d. A DOZEN.

PER DOZEN.	PER GALLON.
Port from .... 15s. to 30s.	Nicholson's Gin 12s. to 13s.
Fine Old ...... 36s. to 60s.	Old Cognac ..24s. to 27s.
Sherries ...... 15s. to 24s.	Finest Pale.......... 30s.
Superior ...... 30s. to 48s.	Pure Whiskies 12s., 18s., and 20s.

Every Article guaranteed of its purity.

———

FULL PRICE LIST FORWARDED OF APPLICATION.

———

Imperial Bottling Stores.

———

BASS' AND ALLSOPP'S ALES.

Quarts—8s. Pints—4s. 6d. Half pints 2s. 6d.

GUINNESS' STOUT.

Quarts—7s. 6d. Pints—4s. Half pints—2s. 6d.

LONDON STOUT.

Quarts — 6s. Pints — 3s. Half pints — 2s.
or in Casks at Brewery Prices.

TETLEY'S SUPERIOR ALES in Casks of all sizes delivered to any part of the Town.

———

E̶ll Bottles and Casks to be returned.

———

̶nilies waited on daily if required.

Price One Shilling, with a plan of Whitby.

TENTH EDITION.

REED'S GUIDE TO WHITBY,

And Visitor's Hand Book of the Town and Neighbourhood.

WHITBY.

——o——

Visitors will find every accommodation at

MR. R. CHIPCHASE'S

WHITE HORSE AND GRIFFIN HOTEL,

CHURCH-STREET,

WHITBY.

OPPOSITE ST. NICHOLAS-STREET,

T. S. NAYLOR'S

HAIR CUTTING & SHAMPOOING ROOMS,

72, NEWBOROUGH-STREET, SCARBOROUGH.

T. S. N. begs respectfully to call the attention of Ladies and Gentlemen whose hair is weak or falling off, to his

Quinine Hair Balm and Quinine Pomade,

the increasing demand for which shews their superiority over other articles of their class; and warrants his bringing them more especially before the public. Indeed without them no Toilet is really complete.

Prices of the Quinine Hair Balm 5s. per bottle. Quinine Pomade 2s. and 3s. 6d. per Jar.

SCARBOROUGH.

—o+o—

SWAN HOTEL, REDCAR.

FAMILY & COMMERCIAL HOUSE.

THOS. KEAN, Proprietor,

In thanking his numerous patrons for their past support, begs to inform them that he has just completed his extensive alterations, and his Hotel is complete with every comfort for both Visitors and Commercial Gentlemen. Excellent Coffee Room, Commercial Room, and Private Apartments. Table d'Hote daily during the Season at Two o'Clock. Parties visiting this Hotel will find every attention paid to their comfort. An Omnibus from the Hotel meets each Train. A first-class Billiard Table. Smoking Rooms.

Wines, Spirits, Bottled and Draught Ales and Porter of the finest quality.

REDCAR.

Visitors will find every accommodation at the

Crown and Anchor Hotel,

HIGH-STREET,

LAWRENCE THOMPSON,

PROPRIETOR.

Terms 5s. 6d. per day, including attendance.

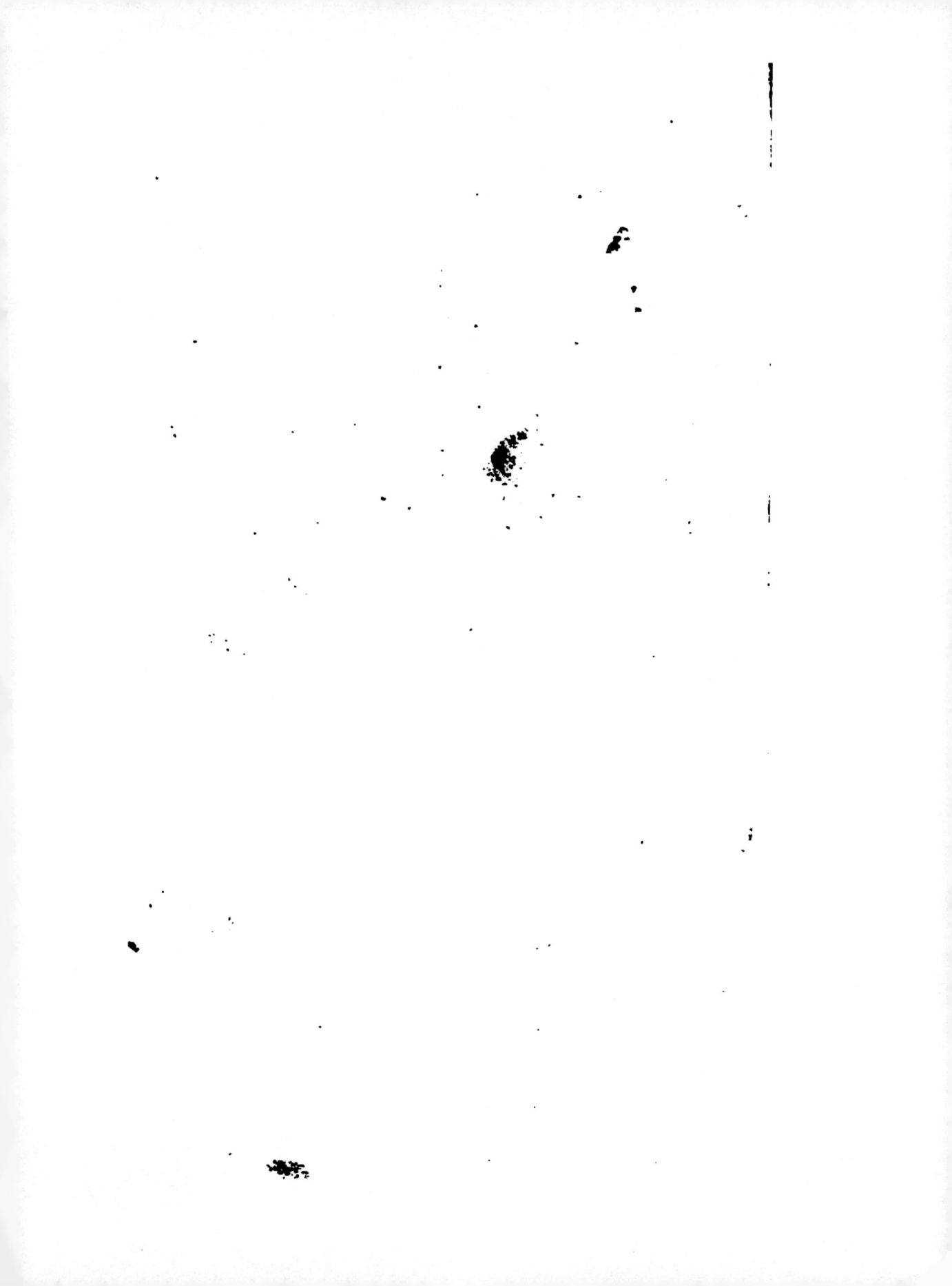

Lightning Source UK Ltd.
Milton Keynes UK
30 November 2010

163673UK00005B/30/P